PowerXL™

AIR FRYER GRILL
COOKBOOK

CREDITS
©2020 RDA Enthusiast Brands, LLC
1610 N. 2nd St., Suite 102, Milwaukee WI
53212-3906
All rights reserved.

International Standard Book Number:
978-1-61765-980-5

Cover photography: Trusted Studios
Eric Theiss portrait: Matt Wagemann

Pictured on front cover:
Grilled Ribeye with Garlic
  Blue Cheese Mustard, p. 122
Air-Fryer Lemon-Parmesan
  Asparagus, p. 147
Air-Fryer Sweet Potato Fries, p. 152
Spinach Tomato Burgers, p. 130
Cilantro-Lime Shrimp, p. 114

Pictured on back cover:
Rotisserie Pork Loin, p. 105
Chocolate Chip Cookie Brownies, p. 192
Fruity Skewers, p. 218

Printed in China
3 5 7 9 10 8 6 4 2

Your Kitchen Game Changer

Home cooks can breathe a sigh of relief. A lot of helpful appliances are out there these days, from slow cookers and electric pressure cookers to air fryers and countertop convection ovens. We all have busy schedules but still crave the time and an easy way to prepare tasty, home-cooked meals for our families. So the variety of options comes in handy for sure.

But let's be honest. Few of us have the space to store all that gear, which is why I'm so excited about the PowerXL Air Fryer Grill. Given the reliability of the PowerXL brand, you know right off the bat that this appliance does two things really well: air-fry your favorite foods, and grill steaks, burgers and other meats indoors, year-round.

That's just the start.

You can grill a perfect steak and air-fry onion rings or another veggie side dish—simultaneously—to create a full meal. And by full, I mean your family will be "full," because the grill pans and crisper trays that come with the PowerXL Air Fryer Grill are purposefully designed for high-volume cooking.

The PowerXL Air Fryer Grill makes cooking healthier, too. Superheated hot air is activated to fry chicken, potatoes, mushrooms and other favorites with 70% less fat than traditional frying methods. Besides cutting calories, this combination of intuitive heating and high-speed air flow also helps reduce cooking time for juicier, more evenly cooked, crispier-than-ever results.

And those are just two cooking functions. The PowerXL Air Fryer Grill actually offers eight ways to cook your favorite recipes. Besides using it to air-fry and grill, you can toast and bake. Roast and reheat. Use it as a pizza oven. Give it a whirl as a rotisserie, and you'll no longer have to pay top dollar for a precooked chicken at the grocery store.

The recipes we've assembled in this PowerXL Air Fryer Grill cookbook take full advantage of the features and functions of your new appliance. We know how crazy life can get. But we also know how satisfying (and fun!) it is to prepare a home-cooked meal. With your PowerXL Air Fryer Grill and this companion cookbook, you have everything you need. So enjoy. And happy cooking.

Eric Theiss
Chef

Cook to the Max!

OUR TEST KITCHEN PROS SHARE THESE TIPS FOR GETTING THE MOST OUT OF YOUR POWERXL AIR FRYER GRILL.

CUT FOOD TO FIT

The basket for air frying sits near the top of the appliance, so be sure the chicken, potatoes, mushrooms or other foods you're cooking are no taller than 2½ inches.

CLEVER CLEANUP

Resist the temptation to line the Drip Tray with aluminum foil to make cleanup easier—it will cause the unit to overheat. Instead, remove baked-on gunk by making a paste of baking soda (a base) and vinegar or lemon juice (an acid). Apply the paste and allow the tray to sit for about 20 minutes before wiping the Drip Tray clean with a damp towel.

EASY DOES IT

Use oven mitts to slide plates and trays into their correct position. To prevent the accessories from sliding out of the PowerXL Air Fryer Grill, never pull them more than halfway out.

AIR-FRY FEARLESSLY

Here's good news for cheeseburger lovers: The fan in the PowerXL Air Fryer Grill is gentler than that of other air fryers. Lighter-weight foods (like a slice of sharp cheddar), which otherwise may fly around, fare well in this machine.

GO LONG

Use long-handled tongs to easily add, flip or remove food from the PowerXL Air Fryer Grill plates and tray.

GRILL SMART

To ensure nice grill marks on steaks, chicken and other meats, pat the foods dry before placing them on the plate. Foods that are wet or in a marinade will cook just fine in the PowerXL Air Fryer Grill, but you might not get those coveted marks.

CRISP DECISIONS

Use the Air Fry Function to get leftovers like pizza and chicken crispy again.

ENJOY EXPERIMENTING

The Baking Tray works great for roasting vegetables—and the Griddle Plate works even better! Veggies cooked on the Griddle Plate get a more roasted color and a crispier texture. Another clever use of a PowerXL Air Fryer Grill accessory? Make pancakes in the Egg Tray. They get super fluffy and you can make four at a time versus two on the Griddle Plate. There's no need to preheat the tray; just fill it with circles of batter, cook until bubbles form, then flip to finish cooking. Try silicone tongs to make flipping easier.

MIX & MATCH

Use the Grill Plate like a roasting rack when cooking items like bacon or a whole chicken. The drippings gather in the bottom, and the food above crisps nicely.

Breakfast by the Batch

Air-Fryer Breakfast Cookies

INGREDIENTS

1	cup mashed ripe bananas (about 2 medium)
½	cup chunky peanut butter
½	cup honey
1	tsp. vanilla extract
1	cup old-fashioned oats
½	cup whole wheat flour
¼	cup nonfat dry milk powder
2	tsp. ground cinnamon
½	tsp. salt
¼	tsp. baking soda
1	cup dried cranberries or raisins

DIRECTIONS

In a large bowl, beat bananas, peanut butter, honey and vanilla until blended. In another bowl, combine oats, flour, milk powder, cinnamon, salt and baking soda; gradually beat into the banana mixture. Stir in dried cranberries.

Slide the Pizza Rack into Shelf Position 4. In batches, drop dough by ¼ cupfuls 2 in. apart onto greased Baking Pan; flatten to ½-in. thickness.

Place the Baking Pan on the Pizza Rack. Turn Function Dial to Air Fry, set temperature to 300° and set timer to 8 minutes. Cook until lightly browned, 6-8 minutes. Cool on Baking Pan 1 minute. Remove to wire racks.

Serve warm or at room temperature.

Freeze option Freeze cookies in freezer containers, separating layers with waxed paper. To use, thaw before serving or, if desired, air fry at 300° until warmed, about 1 minute.

1 COOKIE *212 cal., 6g fat (1g sat. fat), 0 chol., 186mg sod., 38g carb. (25g sugars, 4g fiber), 5g pro.*

PREP 20 min.   **COOK** 10 min./batch   **SERVES** 12

Air-Fryer Ham & Egg Pockets

INGREDIENTS

- 1 large egg
- 2 tsp. 2% milk
- 2 tsp. butter
- 1 oz. thinly sliced deli ham, chopped
- 2 Tbsp. shredded cheddar cheese
- 1 tube (4 oz.) refrigerated crescent rolls

DIRECTIONS

In a small bowl, combine egg and milk. In a small skillet, heat butter until hot. Add egg mixture; cook and stir over medium heat until eggs are completely set. Remove from the heat. Fold in ham and cheese.

Separate crescent dough into 2 rectangles. Seal perforations; spoon half the filling down the center of each rectangle. Fold dough over filling; pinch to seal.

Place pockets in a single layer on greased Crisper Tray and insert into Shelf Position 4. Turn the Function Dial to Air Fry, set temperature to 300° and set timer to 10 minutes. Cook until golden brown, 8-10 minutes.

1 SERVING *326 cal., 20g fat (5g sat. fat), 118mg chol., 735mg sod., 25g carb. (6g sugars, 0 fiber), 12g pro.*

TAKES 25 min.   **SERVES** 2

Sheet-Pan Smarts

Corral food-prep ingredients with a handy sheet pan or tray. It keeps you organized and speeds cleanup. Sheet pans also help contain messy tasks like breading.

Air-Fryer Puff Pastry Danishes

INGREDIENTS

- 1 pkg. (8 oz.) cream cheese, softened
- ¼ cup sugar
- 2 Tbsp. all-purpose flour
- ½ tsp. vanilla extract
- 2 large egg yolks, divided use
- 1 Tbsp. water
- 1 pkg. (17.3 oz.) frozen puff pastry, thawed
- ⅔ cup seedless raspberry jam or jam of choice

DIRECTIONS

In a large bowl, beat cream cheese, sugar, flour and vanilla until smooth; beat in 1 egg yolk.

Mix water and remaining egg yolk. On a lightly floured surface, unfold each sheet of puff pastry; roll into a 12-in. square. Cut each into nine 4-in. squares.

Top each square with 1 Tbsp. cream cheese mixture and 1 rounded tsp. jam. Bring 2 opposite corners of pastry over filling, sealing with yolk mixture. Brush tops with remaining yolk mixture.

In batches, place pastries in a single layer on greased Crisper Tray and insert into Shelf Position 4. Turn the Function Dial to Air Fry, set the temperature to 325° and set the timer to 10 minutes.

Cook until golden brown, 8-10 minutes. Serve warm. Refrigerate leftovers.

1 PASTRY *197 cal., 12g fat (4g sat. fat), 33mg chol., 130mg sod., 20g carb. (3g sugars, 2g fiber), 3g pro.*

PREP 25 min.   **COOK** 10 min./batch   **SERVES** 18

Bacon Pot Pie

INGREDIENTS

  2 cups all-purpose flour
 ⅓ cup shortening
 ¼ cup cold butter
  5 to 7 Tbsp. ice water

FILLING

  2 medium red potatoes, chopped
  1 Tbsp. water
  2 Tbsp. butter
  3 Tbsp. all-purpose flour
  2 cups 2% milk
 ¼ tsp. garlic powder
 ¼ tsp. pepper
  1 lb. bacon strips, cooked and
     crumbled
  1 medium onion, chopped
  1 cup chopped fresh or frozen
     broccoli, thawed
  1 cup shredded cheddar cheese

Good Grease

Bacon grease is so tasty, it's worth saving for other dishes. Once it's slightly cooled, strain the grease through cheesecloth or a coffee filter. Cover and refrigerate cooled grease up to 6 months. Cook your morning eggs and potato dishes in the bacon grease. Want a real treat? Use it for popping corn, and relish the delicate flavor.

DIRECTIONS

Place flour in a large bowl; cut in shortening and butter until crumbly. Gradually add ice water 1 Tbsp. at a time, tossing with a fork until dough holds together when pressed. Divide dough in half. Shape each into a disk; wrap and refrigerate 1 hour or overnight.

In a microwave-safe bowl, combine potatoes and water; microwave, covered, on high until tender, 4-5 minutes. Cool; drain. In a small saucepan, melt butter over medium heat. Stir in flour until smooth; gradually whisk in milk, garlic powder and pepper. Bring to a boil, stirring constantly; cook and stir until thickened, 2-3 minutes. Cool and set aside.

On a lightly floured surface, roll half the dough to a ⅛-in.-thick circle; transfer to a 9-in. deep-dish pie plate. Trim even with rim. Place potatoes in crust. Top with bacon, onion, broccoli and cheese. Pour sauce over top. Roll remaining dough to a ⅛-in.-thick circle. Place over filling. Trim, seal and flute edge. Cut slits in top. Place on the Baking Pan.

Slide the Pizza Rack into Shelf Position 5. Place the Baking Pan on the Pizza Rack. Turn Function Dial to Pizza/Bake, set temperature to 375° and set the timer to 60 minutes. Bake until crust is golden brown and filling is bubbly, 50-60 minutes. Let stand 10 minutes.

1 PIECE *493 cal., 31g fat (14g sat. fat), 62mg chol., 558mg sod., 36g carb. (4g sugars, 2g fiber), 17g pro.*

PREP 30 min.   **COOK** 50 min.   **SERVES** 8

Breakfast Skewers

INGREDIENTS

- 1 pkg. (7 oz.) frozen fully cooked breakfast sausage links, thawed
- 1 can (20 oz.) pineapple chunks, drained
- 10 medium fresh mushrooms
- 2 Tbsp. butter, melted
- Maple syrup

DIRECTIONS

Cut sausages in half; on 5 metal or soaked wooden skewers, alternately thread sausages, pineapple and mushrooms. Brush with butter and syrup.

Slide the Grill Plate into Shelf Position 6. Turn the Function Dial to Grill, set temperature to 350° and set timer to 20 minutes. Let the grill preheat for 10 minutes.

When the grill has preheated, place skewers on the Grill Plate. Cook, basting occasionally with syrup, until lightly browned and fruit is heated through, 4-5 minutes on each side.

1 SKEWER *246 cal., 20g fat (8g sat. fat), 37mg chol., 431mg sod., 13g carb. (12g sugars, 1g fiber), 7g pro.*

TAKES 20 min.   **SERVES** 5

Coastal Carolina Muffin-Tin Frittatas

INGREDIENTS

- 3 Tbsp. mayonnaise
- 1 tsp. lemon juice
- ½ tsp. sugar
- ¼ tsp. seafood seasoning
- ⅔ cup refrigerated shredded hash brown potatoes
- ⅔ cup jumbo lump crabmeat
- ½ cup chopped smoked sausage
- 2 Tbsp. chopped roasted sweet red peppers
- 3 large eggs
- ¼ cup heavy whipping cream
- 1 tsp. Louisiana-style hot sauce
- ¼ tsp. salt
- 3 bacon strips, cooked and crumbled
  Thinly sliced green onions

DIRECTIONS

In a small bowl, combine the mayonnaise, lemon juice, sugar and seafood seasoning. Refrigerate until serving.

Meanwhile, in a large bowl, combine the potatoes, crab, sausage and red peppers. Divide among cups of a greased 6-cup muffin tin that fits in the unit. In another large bowl, whisk the eggs, cream, hot sauce and salt. Pour over potato mixture. Top with bacon.

Slide the Pizza Rack into Shelf Position 5. Place the muffin tin on the Pizza Rack. Turn the Function Dial to Bake, set temperature to 350° and set timer to 30 minutes. Bake until a knife inserted in center comes out clean, 30-35 minutes. Serve with sauce and sliced green onions.

1 FRITTATA *292 cal., 23g fat (8g sat. fat), 164mg chol., 768mg sod., 7g carb. (2g sugars, 1g fiber), 13g pro.*

PREP 25 min.   **BAKE** 30 min.   **SERVES** 6

BAKE

Dulce de Leche French Toast Bake

INGREDIENTS

- 8 slices Texas toast
- ⅓ cup whipped cream cheese
- ⅓ cup dulce de leche
- 3 large eggs
- ½ cup 2% milk
- ½ cup half-and-half cream
- 3 Tbsp. sugar
- 1½ tsp. vanilla extract

TOPPING
- ½ cup packed brown sugar
- ¼ cup butter, cubed
- 1 Tbsp. corn syrup
- ¾ cup chopped pecans

DIRECTIONS

Slide the Pizza Rack into Shelf Position 2. Place 4 slices of Texas toast on the Pizza Rack. Turn the Function Dial to Toast and set temperature to 300°. Toast until light brown. Repeat with remaining Texas toast.

Arrange half of the toast in a single layer in a greased 8-in. square baking pan that fits in the unit, trimming to fit into dish if necessary. In a small bowl, mix cream cheese and dulce de leche; spread over toast. Top with remaining toast.

In a small bowl, whisk the eggs, milk, cream, sugar and vanilla; pour over toast. Refrigerate, covered, overnight.

Remove pan from refrigerator 30 minutes prior to baking. In a small saucepan, combine brown sugar, butter and corn syrup; cook and stir over medium heat until sugar is dissolved. Stir in pecans; spread over top.

Slide the Pizza Rack into Shelf Position 5. Place the baking pan on the Pizza Rack. Turn the Function Dial to Pizza/Bake, set temperature to 350° and set timer to 50 minutes. Bake until puffed, golden and a knife inserted in the center comes out clean, 40-50 minutes. Let stand 5-10 minutes before cutting.

1 PIECE *551 cal., 28g fat (11g sat. fat), 139mg chol., 434mg sod., 64g carb. (41g sugars, 2g fiber), 11g pro.*

PREP 30 min. + chilling **BAKE** 40 min. **SERVES** 6

HOW TO

Crack an Egg with Ease

Advance your culinary skills and use simple physics to impress your friends and family. With an egg in each hand, crack one egg by hitting it against the other. Like magic, the second egg won't break. Use your fingers to split open the eggshell. Pour the yolk and egg white into a bowl. Crack the final egg against the countertop.

Egg-Topped Sausage Herb Pizza

INGREDIENTS

- 1 Tbsp. sugar
- 2 tsp. quick-rise yeast
- ½ tsp. salt
- 1 to 1½ cups all-purpose flour
- ½ cup water
- 2 Tbsp. olive oil
- 1¼ tsp. Italian seasoning
- 2 Tbsp. cornmeal
- 2 hot Italian sausage links (4 oz. each), casings removed
- ¾ cup pizza sauce
- 1½ cups shredded part-skim mozzarella cheese
- 4 large eggs
- ¼ tsp. pepper
- ¼ cup grated Parmesan cheese
- ¼ cup grated Romano cheese
- ½ cup fresh arugula or baby spinach
- ½ cup fresh baby spinach

DIRECTIONS

In a small bowl, mix sugar, yeast, salt and ¾ cup flour. In a small saucepan, heat water and oil to 120°-130°; stir into dry ingredients. Stir in Italian seasoning and enough remaining flour to form a soft dough (dough will be sticky). Turn the dough onto a floured surface; knead until smooth and elastic, 6-8 minutes. Place in a greased bowl, turning once to grease top. Cover and let rise in a warm place until doubled, about 45 minutes.

Grease Grill Plate; sprinkle with cornmeal. Meanwhile, in a small skillet, cook sausage over medium heat 4-5 minutes or until no longer pink, breaking into crumbles; drain.

Roll dough to fit Grill Plate; pinch edge to form a rim. Spread with pizza sauce; top with sausage and the mozzarella cheese. Turn Function Dial to Pizza/Bake, set temperature to 450° and set timer to 5 minutes. Preheat oven. Slide Grill Plate into Shelf Position 6. Bake until crust is lightly browned, 7-8 minutes.

Remove Grill Plate. Using the back of a tablespoon, make 4 indentations in pizza at least 2 in. from edge. Carefully break an egg into each indentation; sprinkle with pepper and Parmesan and Romano cheeses. Return and bake until egg whites are completely set and yolks begin to thicken but are not hard, 4-5 minutes. Before serving, top with arugula and spinach.

1 SLICE *339 cal., 21g fat (8g sat. fat), 131mg chol., 729mg sod., 20g carb. (3g sugars, 1g fiber), 17g pro.*

| **PREP** 45 min. + rising | **BAKE** 15 min. | **SERVES** 8 |

HACK IT! Not Just for Slicing Pizza

The wheel of a pizza cutter works in both directions, making it ideal for chopping herbs. Bunch up the herbs and run the cutter back and forth until they're chopped as desired.

Ham & Cheese Grits Casserole

INGREDIENTS

- 3 cups chicken stock
- 1 cup quick-cooking grits
- ½ cup Southwestern-style egg substitute
- 5 oz. reduced-fat Velveeta, cubed
- ¼ cup 2% milk
- 2 Tbsp. butter
- 1¼ cups cubed fully cooked ham
- 3 green onions, chopped
- ¼ tsp. salt
- ¼ tsp. garlic powder
- ¼ tsp. pepper
- ⅛ to ¼ tsp. crushed red pepper flakes
- ¾ cup shredded cheddar cheese

DIRECTIONS

In a large saucepan, bring chicken stock to a boil. Slowly stir in grits. Reduce heat to medium-low; cook, covered, about 5 minutes or until thickened, stirring occasionally. Remove from heat. In a small bowl, stir a small amount of hot grits into egg substitute; return all to pan, mixing well.

Add Velveeta, milk and butter; stir until cheese is melted. Stir in ham, green onions and seasonings. Transfer to a greased 11x7-in. baking dish that fits into the unit. Sprinkle with cheddar cheese.

Slide the Pizza Rack into Shelf Position 5. Place the baking dish on the Pizza Rack. Turn the Function Dial to Pizza/Bake, set temperature to 350° and set timer to 40 minutes. Bake until edges are golden brown and cheese is melted, 35-40 minutes. Let stand 10 minutes before serving.

1 PIECE *284 cal., 12g fat (7g sat. fat), 51mg chol., 1212mg sod., 26g carb. (3g sugars, 1g fiber), 20g pro.*

PREP 30 min.   **BAKE** 35 min. + standing   **SERVES** 6

Spiced Apricot Baked Oatmeal

INGREDIENTS

- ¾ cup packed brown sugar
- 3 tsp. pumpkin pie spice
- 2 tsp. baking powder
- ½ tsp. salt
- ¼ tsp. ground cardamom
- 3 cups old-fashioned oats
- ½ cup chopped dried apricots
- ½ cup chopped pecans, toasted
- 3 large eggs
- 1½ cups fat-free milk
- ½ cup unsweetened applesauce
- 1½ tsp. vanilla extract
- ¼ cup butter, melted

TOPPINGS
- 3 cups vanilla yogurt
- ½ cup apricot preserves, warmed

DIRECTIONS

Preheat oven to 350°. In a large bowl, mix the first 5 ingredients; stir in oats, apricots and pecans. In another bowl, whisk together eggs, milk, applesauce and vanilla; gradually whisk in melted butter. Stir into oat mixture. Transfer to a greased 11x7-in. baking dish that fits into the unit.

Slide the Pizza Rack into Shelf Position 5. Place the baking dish on the Pizza Rack. Turn the Function Dial to Pizza/Bake, set temperature to 350° and set timer to 30 minutes. Bake until set and edges are lightly browned, 25-30 minutes. Cut into 12 portions; serve with toppings.

1 PIECE WITH ¼ CUP YOGURT AND 2 TSP. PRESERVES
327 cal., 11g fat (4g sat. fat), 60mg chol., 280mg sod., 52g carb. (33g sugars, 3g fiber), 9g pro.

PREP 15 min.   **BAKE** 25 min.   **SERVES** 12

Freeze Ease
Save some oatmeal for later! Freeze cooled portions in airtight freezer containers. Reheat by popping them back into the PowerXL Air Fryer Grill, warming for 4-5 minutes or until heated through. Serve with toppings.

Cook-and-Go Lunches

Bacon Swiss Quiche

INGREDIENTS

- 1 sheet refrigerated pie crust
- ¼ cup sliced green onions
- 1 Tbsp. butter
- 6 large eggs
- 1½ cups heavy whipping cream
- ¼ cup unsweetened apple juice
- 1 lb. sliced bacon, cooked and crumbled
- ⅛ tsp. salt
- ⅛ tsp. pepper
- 2 cups shredded Swiss cheese

DIRECTIONS

Unroll crust into a 9-in. pie plate that fits in the unit; trim and flute edges. Set aside. In a small skillet, saute green onions in butter until tender.

In a large bowl, whisk eggs, cream and juice. Stir in bacon, salt, pepper and sauteed onions. Pour into crust; sprinkle with cheese.

Slide the Pizza Rack into Shelf Position 5. Place the pie plate on the Pizza Rack. Turn the Function Dial to Bake, set the temperature to 350° and set the timer to 40 minutes. Bake until a knife inserted in the center comes out clean, 35-40 minutes. Let stand 10 minutes before cutting.

Freeze option Securely wrap individual portions of cooled quiche in parchment and foil; freeze. To use, partially thaw in refrigerator overnight. Slide the Pizza Rack into Shelf Position 5. Unwrap and arrange quiche on Baking Pan; place Baking Pan on Pizza Rack. Turn the Function Dial to Reheat, set temperature to 350° and set timer to 15 minutes. Cook until heated through and a thermometer inserted in center reads 165°.

1 PIECE *739 cal., 60g fat (31g sat. fat), 359mg chol., 781mg sod., 22g carb. (4g sugars, 0 fiber), 27g pro.*

PREP 15 min.   **BAKE** 35 min. + standing   **SERVES** 6

Beef Pasties

INGREDIENTS

2 cups cubed cooked roast beef
(¼-in. pieces)
1½ cup finely chopped cooked
potatoes
1 cup beef gravy
½ cup finely chopped carrot
½ cup finely chopped cooked onion
1 Tbsp. chopped fresh parsley
¼ tsp. dried thyme
½ tsp. salt
⅛ to ¼ tsp. pepper
Pastry for double-crust pie (9 in.)
Half-and-half cream

DIRECTIONS

In a large bowl, combine the first 9 ingredients; set aside. On a lightly floured surface, roll out 1 portion of dough into an 8-in. circle. Mound 1 cup filling on half of circle. Moisten edges with water; fold crust over filling and press the edges with a fork to seal.

Place on ungreased Baking Pan. Repeat with the remaining dough and filling. Cut slits in top of each; brush with cream.

Slide the Pizza Rack into Shelf Position 5. Place the Baking Pan on the Pizza Rack. Turn Function Dial to Pizza/Bake, set temperature to 450° and set timer for 20 minutes. Bake until golden brown, 15-20 minutes.

1 SERVING *724 cal., 33g fat (14g sat. fat), 93mg chol., 1057mg sod., 71g carb. (6g sugars, 2g fiber), 33g pro.*

PREP 20 min. **BAKE** 15 min. **SERVES** 4

HOW TO

Make Pastry for Double-Crust Pie

Combine 2½ cups all-purpose flour and ½ tsp. salt; cut in 1 cup cold butter until crumbly. Gradually add ⅓ to ⅔ cup ice water, tossing with a fork until dough holds together when pressed. Divide dough into quarters. Shape each into a disk; wrap and refrigerate 1 hour or overnight.

Buffalo Chicken Biscuits

INGREDIENTS

- 1½ cups chopped rotisserie chicken
- 2 Tbsp. Louisiana-style hot sauce
- 1 cup biscuit/baking mix
- ⅛ tsp. celery seed
  Dash pepper
- 2 Tbsp. lightly beaten egg
- ¼ cup 2% milk
- 2 Tbsp. ranch salad dressing
- ¾ cup shredded Colby-Monterey Jack cheese, divided
- 1 green onion, thinly sliced
  Optional: Additional ranch dressing and hot sauce

DIRECTIONS

Toss chicken with hot sauce. In a small bowl, whisk together baking mix, celery seed and pepper. In another bowl, whisk together egg, milk and ranch dressing; add to dry ingredients, stirring just until moistened. Fold in ½ cup cheese, green onion and chicken mixture.

Spoon into a greased 6-cup muffin tin that fits in the unit. Sprinkle with remaining cheese. Slide the Pizza Rack into Shelf Position 2 and place the muffin tin on the Pizza Rack. Turn the Function Dial to Pizza/Bake, set temperature to 400° and set timer for 20 minutes. Bake until a toothpick inserted in center comes out clean, 15-20 minutes.

Cool 5 minutes before removing from pan to a wire rack. Serve warm. If desired, serve with additional dressing and hot sauce. Refrigerate leftovers.

1 MUFFIN *230cal., 12g fat (5g sat. fat), 61mg chol., 590mg sod., 15g carb. (2g sugars, 1g fiber), 16g pro.*

PREP 20 min.　　**BAKE** 15 min.　　**SERVES** 6

Go Mild
The best way to let the bold flavors of this savory recipe shine is to go with a milder rotisserie glaze like the Citrus Apricot Glaze on page 93.

ROAST

Honey-Lime Roasted Chicken

INGREDIENTS

1 whole roasting chicken (5 to 6 lbs.)
¼ cup lime juice
2 Tbsp. honey
1 Tbsp. stone-ground mustard or spicy brown mustard
1 tsp. salt
1 tsp. ground cumin

DIRECTIONS

Carefully loosen the skin from the entire chicken. Place chicken on Grill Plate. Whisk lime juice, honey, mustard, salt and cumin. Using a turkey baster, baste under the chicken skin with half the lime juice mixture. Tie drumsticks together. Brush chicken with additional lime mixture.

Slide the Grill Plate into Shelf Position 6. Turn the Function Dial to Pizza/Bake, set the temperature to 350° and set the timer to 90 minutes; roast until a thermometer inserted in thickest part of thigh reads 170°-175°, 1-1½ hours. (Cover loosely with foil if chicken browns too quickly.) Let stand for 10 minutes before carving.

4 OZ. COOKED CHICKEN *294 cal., 16g fat (4g sat. fat), 90mg chol., 354mg sod., 8g carb. (7g sugars, 0 fiber), 28g pro.*

PREP 10 min. **BAKE** 1 hour + standing **SERVES** 10

HACK IT!

Double Down
It takes less than an hour to cook a rotisserie chicken in the PowerXL Air Fryer Grill. So roast two chickens back to back to double up on delicious recipes like this one!

GRILL

Mandarin-Berry Steak Salad

INGREDIENTS

- ¾ lb. beef sirloin steak
- 1 tsp. salt, divided
- ¼ tsp. pepper
- 3 Tbsp. olive oil
- ¼ cup cider vinegar
- ¼ cup orange juice
- 2 Tbsp. minced fresh parsley
- 2 Tbsp. honey
- 1 garlic clove, minced
- 1 tsp. chili sauce
- 8 cups torn romaine
- 3 cups sliced fresh strawberries
- 1 small red onion, sliced
- 1 can (11 oz.) mandarin oranges, drained
- ½ cup chopped pecans, toasted
- 2 oz. fresh goat cheese, crumbled

DIRECTIONS

Slide the Grill Plate into Shelf Position 6. Turn the Function Dial to Grill, set the temperature to 450° and set the timer to 25 minutes. Preheat the grill for 10 minutes. Sprinkle steak with ½ tsp. salt and pepper.

When the grill has preheated, place the steak on Grill Plate. Cook until the desired doneness is reached (5-6 minutes per side for medium). Let rest 5 minutes before slicing.

Meanwhile, in a small bowl, whisk the oil, vinegar, juice, parsley, honey, garlic, chili sauce and remaining ½ tsp. salt; set aside. Divide romaine among 4 plates; top with steak, strawberries, onion, oranges, pecans and cheese. Serve with vinaigrette.

1 SERVING *443 cal., 24g fat (4g sat. fat), 46mg chol., 367mg sod., 40g carb. (31g sugars, 7g fiber), 21g pro.*

TAKES 25 min.   **SERVES** 4

HOW TO

Hull a Strawberry
Insert a straw into the berry's tip and push the hull through the other end.

Summer Chicken Macaroni Salad

INGREDIENTS

- 1½ cups uncooked elbow macaroni
- 1 rotisserie chicken (page 94), skin removed, meat shredded
- ¾ cup fresh or frozen peas
- 5 green onions, finely chopped
- 2 celery ribs, thinly sliced
- ⅓ cup loosely packed basil leaves, thinly sliced
- ¼ cup lemon juice, divided
- 1 teaspoon kosher salt
- ¾ teaspoon coarsely ground pepper
- ¾ cup plain yogurt
- ¾ cup reduced-fat mayonnaise
- 3 medium peaches, peeled and sliced
- 1 cup sharp cheddar cheese, shredded
- ½ cup crumbled Gorgonzola cheese
- ¾ cup pistachios

DIRECTIONS

Cook macaroni according to the package directions. Meanwhile, mix chicken, peas, onions, celery, basil, 2 Tbsp. lemon juice, salt and pepper. Drain macaroni; rinse with cold water, then drain again. Add to chicken mixture. Mix yogurt, mayonnaise and the remaining lemon juice. Add to salad and mix well. Add peaches and cheeses; toss gently. Refrigerate at least 2 hours. Sprinkle with pistachios before serving.

¾ **CUP** 312 cal., 16g fat (5g sat. fat), 85mg chol., 379mg sod., 13g carb. (5g sugars, 2g fiber), 29g pro.

PREP 25 min. + chilling   **SERVES** 16

PRO TIP!

A Cut Above
Slicing green onions thinly on the diagonal is an easy way to give them a delicate, professional look.

Spicy Peanut Butter & Pork Sandwiches

INGREDIENTS

1	pork tenderloin (¾ lb.)
½	tsp. salt
¼	tsp. pepper
¾	cup creamy peanut butter
12	slices crusty white bread
¼	cup Sriracha chili sauce
	Curry powder
	Thinly sliced jalapeno pepper

DIRECTIONS

Slide the Grill Plate into Shelf Position 6. Turn the Function Dial to Air Fry/Grill, set temperature to 400° and set timer to 30 minutes. Preheat the grill for 10 minutes. Sprinkle pork with salt and pepper.

When the grill is preheated, place the pork on the Grill Plate. Cook until a thermometer reads 145°, 15-20 minutes. Remove roast to cutting board. Let stand 5 minutes. Shred pork with 2 forks.

Spread 1 Tbsp. peanut butter over each slice of bread. Layer with pork and 1 tsp. chili sauce. Sprinkle with curry powder; top with jalapeno.

1 OPEN-FACED SANDWICH *215 cal., 11g fat (2g sat. fat), 16mg chol., 381mg sod., 20g carb. (5g sugars, 2g fiber), 11g pro.*

PREP 20 min.   **COOK** 15 min.   **SERVES** 12

Flip It Good

To make natural or homemade peanut butter super easy to mix, store the jar upside down. Flip the jar right-side up and the oil, which will have settled to the "bottom" of the jar, will rise back to the top and will incorporate more smoothly.

Spinach & Cheese Lasagna Rolls

INGREDIENTS

- 1 pkg. (10 oz.) frozen chopped spinach, thawed and squeezed dry
- 1 cup shredded part-skim mozzarella cheese
- 1 cup 2% cottage cheese
- ¾ cup grated Parmesan cheese, divided
- 1 large egg, lightly beaten
- 6 lasagna noodles, cooked and drained
- 1 jar (24 oz.) marinara sauce

DIRECTIONS

In a small bowl, combine the spinach, mozzarella, cottage cheese, ½ cup Parmesan cheese and egg. Spread a heaping ⅓ cupful over each noodle. Roll up; place seam side down in a greased 9-in. square baking dish that fits in unit. Cover and refrigerate overnight.

Remove from the refrigerator 30 minutes before baking. Pour marinara sauce over roll-ups. Cover with foil.

Slide the Pizza Rack into Shelf Position 5. Place the baking dish on the Pizza Rack. Turn the Function Dial to Bake, set the temperature to 350° and set the timer to 30 minutes. Bake until bubbly, 25-30 minutes. Sprinkle with remaining Parmesan cheese.

1 LASAGNA ROLL *301 cal., 11g fat (5g sat. fat), 56mg chol., 963mg sod., 33g carb. (9g sugars, 4g fiber), 18g pro.*

PREP 25 min. + chilling **BAKE** 25 min. **SERVES** 6

Tomato Power
Vitamins A and C, found in tomatoes, provide vital immune system support, so this dish may boost your health and energy.

Turkey & Broccoli Pastry Braid

INGREDIENTS

- **1** cup finely chopped cooked turkey (about 5 oz.)
- **½** cup finely chopped fresh broccoli
- **½** cup finely chopped sweet red pepper
- **½** cup shredded cheddar cheese
- **¼** cup Miracle Whip
- **¼** tsp. dill weed
- **1** sheet frozen puff pastry, thawed

DIRECTIONS

For filling, mix first 6 ingredients. Unfold pastry onto a lightly floured surface; roll into a 15x10-in. rectangle.

Spoon filling down center third of rectangle. On each long side, cut 8 strips about 3 in. into the center. Starting at an end, fold alternating strips over filling, pinching ends to join. Transfer braid to Baking Pan.

Slide the Pizza Rack into Shelf Position 5. Place the Baking Pan on the Pizza Rack. Turn the Function Dial to Pizza/Bake, set temperature to 400° and set timer to 20 minutes. Bake until golden brown and filling is heated through, 15-20 minutes.

1 PIECE *463 cal., 26g fat (7g sat. fat), 50mg chol., 435mg sod., 38g carb. (2g sugars, 5g fiber), 18g pro.*

TAKES 30 min.   **SERVES** 4

Finger Foods

Jalapeno Chicken Wraps

INGREDIENTS

- 1 lb. boneless skinless chicken breasts
- 1 Tbsp. garlic powder
- 1 Tbsp. onion powder
- 1 Tbsp. pepper
- 2 tsp. seasoned salt
- 1 tsp. paprika
- 1 small onion, cut into strips
- 15 jalapeno peppers, halved and seeded
- 1 lb. sliced bacon, halved widthwise
  Blue cheese salad dressing

DIRECTIONS

Cut chicken into 2x1½-in. strips. In a small bowl, combine the garlic powder, onion powder, pepper, seasoned salt and paprika. In a large shallow dish, sprinkle chicken with spices; toss to coat. Place a chicken strip and an onion strip in each jalapeno half. Wrap each with a piece of bacon and secure with toothpicks.

Meanwhile, slide the Grill Plate into Shelf Position 6. Turn the Function Dial to Grill, set the temperature to 400° and set the timer to 30 minutes. Preheat the grill for 10 minutes.

When the grill is preheated, in batches, place the peppers on the Grill Plate. Cook until chicken is no longer pink and bacon is crisp, 18-20 minutes, turning once. Serve with blue cheese dressing.

2 PIECES *101 cal., 6g fat (2g sat. fat), 25mg chol., 377mg sod., 2g carb. (0 sugars, 1g fiber), 10g pro.*

PREP 15 min.	**GRILL** 20 min./batch	**SERVES** 15

HACK IT!

Double Duty

Use a grapefruit spoon to core and seed a jalapeno pepper. The spoon's curved shape and serrated edges make it ideal for following the pepper's shape.

Air-Fryer Ravioli

INGREDIENTS

- 1 cup seasoned bread crumbs
- ¼ cup shredded Parmesan cheese
- 2 tsp. dried basil
- ½ cup all-purpose flour
- 2 large eggs, lightly beaten
- 1 pkg. (9 oz.) frozen beef ravioli, thawed
- Cooking spray
- Fresh minced basil, optional
- 1 cup marinara sauce, warmed

DIRECTIONS

In a shallow bowl, mix bread crumbs, Parmesan cheese and basil. Place flour and eggs in separate shallow bowls. Dip ravioli in flour to coat both sides; shake off excess. Dip in eggs, then in crumb mixture, patting to help coating adhere.

In batches, arrange ravioli in a single layer on the Crisper Tray; spritz with cooking spray. Slide Crisper Tray into Shelf Position 4. Turn the Function Dial to Air Fry, set temperature to 350° and set the timer to 8 minutes. Cook until golden brown, about 3 minutes.

Turn ravioli; spritz with cooking spray. Cook until golden brown, 3-4 minutes longer. If desired, immediately sprinkle with basil and additional Parmesan cheese. Serve warm with marinara sauce.

3 PIECES *120 cal., 3g fat (1 sat. fat), 19mg chol., 352mg sod., 18g carb. (3g sugars, 2g fiber), 5g pro.*

PREP 20 min. **COOK** 10 min./batch **SERVES** 6

Sweet Sriracha Wings

INGREDIENTS

- 12 chicken wings (about 3 lbs.)
- 1 Tbsp. canola oil
- 2 tsp. ground coriander
- ½ tsp. garlic salt
- ¼ tsp. pepper

SAUCE
- ¼ cup butter, cubed
- ½ cup orange juice
- ⅓ cup Sriracha chili sauce
- 3 Tbsp. honey
- 2 Tbsp. lime juice
- ¼ cup chopped fresh cilantro

DIRECTIONS

Place chicken wings in a large bowl. Mix oil, coriander, garlic salt and pepper; add to wings and toss to coat. Refrigerate, covered, 2 hours or overnight.

For sauce, in a small saucepan, melt butter. Stir in the orange juice, chili sauce, honey and lime juice until blended.

Slide the Grill Plate into Shelf Position 6. Turn the Function Dial to Grill, set temperature to 450° and set timer to 30 minutes. Preheat the grill for 10 minutes.

When the grill has preheated, place wings on the Grill Plate in batches. Cook until juices run clear, turning occasionally, 15-18 minutes; brush with some of the sauce during the last 5 minutes of grilling. Transfer chicken to a large bowl; add remaining sauce and toss to coat. Sprinkle with cilantro.

1 CHICKEN WING *201 cal., 13g fat (5g sat. fat), 46mg chol., 321mg sod., 8g carb. (7g sugars, 0 fiber), 12g pro.*

PREP 20 min. + marinating	**GRILL** 15 min./batch
	SERVES 12

HOW TO

Wing It!

If you prefer wings cut into sections, place each wing on a cutting board. With a sharp knife, cut between the joint at top of the tip end. Discard tips or use for making broth. Take remaining wing and cut between joints. Proceed with recipe as directed.

Air-Fryer Fiesta Chicken Fingers

INGREDIENTS

- ¾ lb. boneless skinless chicken breasts
- ½ cup buttermilk
- ¼ tsp. pepper
- 1 cup all-purpose flour
- 3 cups corn chips, crushed
- 1 envelope taco seasoning
  Ranch dip or salsa

DIRECTIONS

Pound chicken breasts with a meat mallet to ½-in. thickness. Cut into 1-in.-wide strips.

In a shallow bowl, whisk buttermilk and pepper. Place flour in a separate shallow bowl. Mix corn chips and taco seasoning in a third bowl. Dip chicken in flour to coat both sides; shake off excess. Dip in buttermilk mixture, then in corn chip mixture, patting to help coating adhere.

In batches, arrange chicken in a single layer on the Crisper Tray; spritz with cooking spray. Slide the Crisper Tray into Shelf Position 4. Turn the Function Dial to Air Fry, set the temperature to 400° and set the timer to 15 minutes. Cook, turning once, until coating is golden brown and chicken is no longer pink. Serve with ranch dip or salsa.

1 SERVING *676 cal., 36g fat (6g sat. fat), 47mg chol., 1431mg sod., 60g carb. (4g sugars, 3g fiber), 24g pro.*

PREP 20 min.   **COOK** 15 min./batch   **SERVES** 4

Grilled Bruschetta

INGREDIENTS

- ½ cup balsamic vinegar
- 1½ cups chopped and seeded plum tomatoes
- 2 Tbsp. finely chopped shallot
- 1 Tbsp. minced fresh basil
- 2 tsp. plus 3 Tbsp. olive oil, divided
- 1 garlic clove, minced
- 16 slices French bread baguette (½ in. thick)
  Sea salt
  Grated Parmesan cheese

DIRECTIONS

In a small saucepan, bring vinegar to a boil; cook until liquid is reduced to 3 Tbsp., 8-10 minutes. Remove from heat. Meanwhile, combine tomatoes, shallot, basil, 2 tsp. olive oil and garlic. Cover and refrigerate until serving.

Slide the Grill Plate into Shelf Position 6. Turn the Function Dial to Grill, set the temperature to 400° and set the timer to 15 minutes. Preheat the grill for 5 minutes. Meanwhile, brush remaining olive oil over both sides of baguette slices.

When the grill has preheated, place bread on the Grill Plate. Cook until golden brown, 2-3 minutes on each side. Top toasts with tomato mixture. Drizzle with balsamic syrup; sprinkle with sea salt and Parmesan. Serve immediately.

1 APPETIZER *58 cal., 3g fat (0 sat. fat), 0 chol., 49mg sod., 7g carb. (3g sugars, 0 fiber), 1g pro.*

PREP 30 min. **GRILL** 5 min. **SERVES** 16

Grilled Chicken, Mango & Blue Cheese Tortillas

INGREDIENTS

- 1 boneless skinless chicken breast (8 oz.)
- 1 tsp. blackened seasoning
- ¾ cup plain yogurt
- 1½ tsp. grated lime zest
- 2 Tbsp. lime juice
- ¼ tsp. salt
- ⅛ tsp. pepper
- 1 cup finely chopped peeled mango
- ⅓ cup finely chopped red onion
- 4 flour tortillas (8 in.)
- ½ cup crumbled blue cheese
- 2 Tbsp. minced fresh cilantro

DIRECTIONS

Slide the Grill Plate into Shelf Position 6. Turn the Function Dial to Grill, set temperature to 450° and set timer to 25 minutes. Preheat the grill for 10 minutes. Meanwhile, sprinkle chicken with seasoning.

When the grill has preheated, grease it lightly. Place chicken on the Grill Plate. Cook until a thermometer reads 165°, 6-8 minutes on each side.

Meanwhile, in a small bowl, mix yogurt, lime zest, lime juice, salt and pepper. Cool chicken slightly; finely chop and transfer to a small bowl. Stir in mango and onion.

Working in 2 batches, place the tortillas on the Grill Plate. Return the Grill Plate to Shelf Position 6. Turn the Function Dial to Grill, set the temperature to 450°, and set the timer to 10 minutes. Grill tortillas until puffed, 2-3 minutes. Turn; top with chicken mixture and blue cheese. Grill until bottoms of tortillas are lightly browned, 2-3 minutes. Drizzle with yogurt mixture; sprinkle with cilantro. Cut each tortilla into 4 wedges.

2 WEDGES *171 cal., 6g fat (3g sat. fat), 25mg chol., 330mg sod., 20g carb. (4g sugars, 1g fiber), 10g pro.*

TAKES 30 min.   **SERVES** 8

TRY IT!

Wheat for the Win
Swap flour tortillas with whole wheat ones and enjoy a health boost from twice the fiber.

Santorini Lamb Sliders

INGREDIENTS

1 cup plain Greek yogurt
½ cup shredded peeled cucumber
1¼ tsp. salt, divided
1 lb. ground lamb
1 Tbsp. grated lemon zest
4 garlic cloves, minced and divided
2 tsp. dried oregano
¼ tsp. plus ⅛ tsp. pepper, divided
1 tsp. lemon juice
1 tsp. dill weed
10 mini buns or mini ciabatta buns
10 Bibb lettuce leaves or Boston
   lettuce leaves
1 medium red onion, thinly sliced
1 cup crumbled feta cheese

DIRECTIONS

Line a strainer or colander with 4 layers of cheesecloth or 1 coffee filter; place over a bowl. Place the yogurt in prepared strainer and cover yogurt with sides of cheesecloth. Refrigerate 2-4 hours. Meanwhile, place shredded cucumber in a colander over a plate; sprinkle with ¼ tsp. salt and toss. Let stand 30 minutes.

For burgers, in a large bowl, combine lamb, lemon zest, 2 garlic cloves, oregano, ¾ tsp. salt and ¼ tsp. pepper, mixing lightly but thoroughly. Shape into ten ½-in.-thick patties. Refrigerate 30 minutes.

For sauce, remove yogurt from cheesecloth to a bowl; discard strained liquid. Squeeze cucumber and blot dry with paper towels. Add cucumber, lemon juice, dill, remaining 2 garlic cloves, remaining ¼ tsp. salt and remaining ⅛ tsp. pepper to the yogurt, stirring until combined. Refrigerate until serving.

Slide the Grill Plate into Shelf Position 6. Turn the Function Dial to Grill, set temperature to 450° and set timer to 25 minutes. Let grill preheat for 10 minutes.

When the grill has preheated, place the burgers on the Grill Plate and cook until a thermometer reads 160°, 3-4 minutes on each side. Grill buns, cut sides down, until toasted, 30-60 seconds. Serve burgers on buns with lettuce, red onion, feta and the sauce.

1 SLIDER *228 cal., 12g fat (5g sat. fat), 43mg chol., 531mg sod., 16g carb. (3g sugars, 1g fiber), 14g pro.*

PREP 30 min. + chilling   **GRILL** 10 min.   **SERVES** 10

Grilled Corn Hummus Tostadas

INGREDIENTS

- 4 medium ears sweet corn, husked
- 1 small red onion, cut crosswise into ½-in. slices
- 2 Tbsp. olive oil, divided
- 8 corn tortillas (6 in.)
- 1 container (8 oz.) hummus
- ¼ tsp. ground chipotle pepper
- 1 cup cherry tomatoes, halved
- ½ tsp. salt
- 1 medium ripe avocado, peeled and sliced
- ½ cup crumbled feta cheese
- 1 jalapeno pepper, thinly sliced
  Optional: Lime wedges, fresh cilantro leaves and Mexican hot pepper sauce

DIRECTIONS

Slide the Grill Plate into Shelf Position 6. Turn the Function Dial to Grill, set the temperature to 450° and set the timer to 20 minutes. Preheat the grill for 10 minutes. Brush corn and onion with 1 Tbsp. oil.

When the grill is preheated, place the corn and onion on the Grill Plate. Cook until tender and lightly charred, 5-7 minutes, turning occasionally. Cool slightly.

Brush tortillas with remaining oil. In batches, place tortillas on Grill Plate. Return the Grill Plate to Shelf Position 6. Turn the Function Dial to Grill, set the temperature to 450° and set the timer to 6 minutes. Grill the tortillas until crisp and lightly browned, 2-3 minutes per side.

Cut corn from cobs. Process hummus, chipotle pepper and 2 cups cut corn in a food processor until almost smooth. Coarsely chop the grilled onion; toss with tomatoes, salt and any remaining corn.

Spread hummus mixture over tortillas; top with onion mixture, avocado, cheese and jalapeno. If desired, serve with limes, cilantro and pepper sauce.

2 TOSTADAS *453 cal., 23g fat (5g sat. fat), 8mg chol., 692mg sod., 55g carb. (9g sugars, 12g fiber), 14g pro.*

TAKES 30 min.   **SERVES** 4

Meals Made Easy

AIR FRY **GRILL**

Tilapia & Vegetable Medley Dinner

INGREDIENTS

2 medium Yukon Gold potatoes, cut into ½-in. wedges
2 Tbsp. melted butter, divided
3 large fresh Brussels sprouts, quartered
1 cup fresh sugar snap peas, cut into ½-in. pieces
3 large radishes, thinly sliced
1 small carrot, thinly sliced
½ tsp. plus ⅛ tsp. garlic salt, divided
½ tsp. pepper
2 tilapia fillets (6 oz. each)
2 tsp. minced fresh tarragon or ½ tsp. dried tarragon
1 Tbsp. butter, softened
   Optional: Lemon wedges and tartar sauce

DIRECTIONS

In a large bowl, toss potato wedges and 1 Tbsp. melted butter. Place potatoes on Crisper Tray and slide Crisper Tray into Shelf Position 4. Slide the Grill Plate into Shelf Position 6. Turn the Function Dial to Air Fry/Grill, set the temperature to 450° and set the timer to 20 minutes.

In the same large bowl, toss Brussels spouts, peas, radishes, carrot, ½ tsp. garlic salt, pepper and remaining 1 Tbsp. melted butter. Meanwhile, sprinkle tilapia with tarragon and remaining ⅛ tsp. garlic salt.

When there are 10 minutes left on the timer, add vegetable mixture to potatoes on the Crisper Tray. At the same time, place tilapia on the Grill Plate; dot with softened butter. Cook until fish flakes easily with a fork, turning once, 8-10 minutes. If desired, serve with lemon wedges and tartar sauce.

1 SERVING *554 cal., 19g fat (12g sat. fat), 129mg chol., 865mg sod., 56g carb. (8g sugars, 8g fiber), 41g pro.*

PREP 15 min.   **COOK** 20 min.   **SERVES** 2

HACK IT!

Just Chill
Fish stays freshest when stored on ice. To keep it ice cold without mess or damaging the fish's texture, place frozen gel packs or blue ice blocks in a container, then top with wrapped fish. Place in the meat drawer. Use within a few days. Wash the ice packs with hot soapy water before reuse.

AIR FRY **GRILL**

Chipotle-Lime Shrimp Dinner

INGREDIENTS

- ⅓ cup lime juice
- ¼ cup unsalted butter, melted
- 1 tsp. ground chipotle pepper
- 1 tsp. sea salt, divided
- 1 lb. uncooked shrimp (16-20 per lb.), peeled and deveined
- 1½ lbs. baby red potatoes, cut into ¾-in. cubes
- 1 Tbsp. extra virgin olive oil
- ½ lb. fresh asparagus, trimmed
- ½ lb. Broccolini or broccoli, cut into small florets
- 2 Tbsp. minced fresh cilantro
  Lime wedges

DIRECTIONS

Combine lime juice, melted butter, chipotle and ½ tsp. sea salt. Toss shrimp with half the lime juice mixture; set aside.

Toss potatoes with oil and remaining ½ tsp. salt; add to Crisper Tray. Slide the Crisper Tray into Shelf Position 4. Slide the Griddle Plate into Shelf Position 6. Turn the Function Dial to Air Fry/Grill, set the temperature to 400° and set the timer to 30 minutes.

Toss asparagus and Broccolini with remaining half of lime juice mixture. When there are 15 minutes left on the timer, drain shrimp, discarding extra liquid; add to Crisper Tray on top of potatoes. Place vegetables on the Griddle Plate. Cook until shrimp turn pink and vegetables are tender, 10-15 minutes. Sprinkle with cilantro and serve with lime wedges.

1 SERVING *383 cal., 17g fat (8g sat. fat), 168mg chol., 649mg sod., 37g carb. (3g sugars, 5g fiber), 25g pro.*

| PREP 15 min. | COOK 25 min. | SERVES 4 |

HOW TO

Peel and Devein Shrimp

Pull legs and first section of shell to one side. Continue pulling the shell up around the top and to the side. Pull off shell by tail if desired. Remove black vein running down the back of the shrimp by making a shallow slit with a paring knife along the back. Rinse the shrimp under cold water to remove the vein.

Lemon-Dijon Pork Supper

INGREDIENTS

4 tsp. Dijon mustard

2 tsp. grated lemon zest

1 garlic clove, minced

½ tsp. salt

2 Tbsp. canola oil

1 lb. sweet potatoes (about 2 medium), peeled and cut into ½-in. cubes

1 lb. fresh Brussels sprouts (about 4 cups), halved

4 boneless pork loin chops (6 oz. each)
Coarsely ground pepper, optional

DIRECTIONS

In a large bowl, mix first 4 ingredients; gradually whisk in oil. Remove 1 Tbsp. mixture for brushing pork. Add vegetables to remaining mixture; toss to coat. Place vegetables on the Crisper Tray. Slide the Crisper Tray into Shelf Position 4. Slide the Grill Plate into Shelf Position 6. Turn the Function Dial to Air Fry/Grill, set the temperature to 450°, and set the timer to 40 minutes.

When there are 10 minutes left on the timer, brush chops with reserved mustard mixture and place on the Grill Plate. When there are 5 minutes left on the timer, flip the chops; continue to cook until a thermometer inserted in pork reads 145° and vegetables are tender, about 5 minutes. If desired, sprinkle with pepper. Let stand 5 minutes before serving.

1 SERVING *456 cal., 17g fat (4g sat. fat), 82mg chol., 499mg sod., 37g carb. (14g sugars, 7g fiber), 38g pro.*

PREP 20 min. **COOK** 40 min. **SERVES** 4

HOW TO

Zest a Lemon 3 Ways

Use a rasp–a hand-held grater that makes ready-to-use, superfine zest. Or, using the finest side of a box grater, carefully zest the lemon; be sure not to grate down to the pale-colored pith. With a citrus zester, make narrow strips of zest and then mince finely with a knife.

AIR FRY **GRILL**

Mini Meat Loaf Meal

INGREDIENTS

- 3 large potatoes, peeled and cut into ½-in. pieces
- 3 Tbsp. olive oil, divided
- ¾ tsp. garlic salt, divided
- ¼ tsp. pepper, divided
- 1 lb. fresh asparagus, trimmed
- ¾ cup quick-cooking oats
- ½ cup tomato juice
- 1 large egg, lightly beaten
- ¼ cup finely chopped onion
- ½ tsp. salt
- 1½ lbs. lean ground beef (90% lean)
- ¼ cup ketchup
- 3 Tbsp. brown sugar
- 1 tsp. prepared mustard
  Dash ground nutmeg, optional

HOW TO

Chop an Onion

To quickly chop an onion, peel and cut it in half from the root to the top. Leaving the root attached, place the flat side down on the work surface. Cut vertically through the onion, leaving the root end uncut. Cut across the onion, discarding the root end. The closer the cuts, the more finely the onion will be chopped.

DIRECTIONS

Combine potatoes with 2 Tbsp. oil, ½ tsp. garlic salt and ⅛ tsp. pepper; toss to coat. Add to Crisper Tray in a single layer. Slide the Crisper Tray into Shelf Position 1. Turn the Function Dial to Air Fry/Grill, set temperature to 425° and set the timer to 10 minutes.

While the potatoes cook, combine asparagus with remaining 1 Tbsp. oil, ¼ tsp. garlic salt and ⅛ tsp. pepper; toss to coat. Place on Grill Plate. In a large bowl, combine oats, tomato juice, egg, onion and salt. Add beef; mix lightly but thoroughly. Shape into six 4x2x1-in. loaves; place on Griddle Plate.

After potatoes have cooked for 10 minutes, slide Griddle Plate into Shelf Position 6 and slide Grill Plate into Shelf Position 3. Set the timer for 15 minutes. Combine ketchup, brown sugar, mustard and, if desired, nutmeg; when 15-minute cycle has finished, brush ketchup mixture over loaves. Set timer for 20 minutes and cook until a thermometer inserted into meat loaves reads 160° and vegetables are tender, 15-20 minutes. Let stand 5-10 minutes before serving.

1 MEAT LOAF WITH 1¼ CUPS VEGETABLES *448 cal., 18g fat (5g sat. fat), 102mg chol., 711mg sod., 45g carb. (13g sugars, 4g fiber), 28g pro.*

PREP 25 min. **COOK** 40 min. **SERVES** 6

Portobello & Polenta Dinner

INGREDIENTS

- ¼ cup olive oil
- 2 Tbsp. balsamic vinegar
- 1 Tbsp. minced fresh oregano
- ¾ tsp. garlic powder
- ½ tsp. salt
- ¼ tsp. pepper
- 1 tube (18 oz.) polenta, cut into 8 slices
- 4 large portobello mushrooms (4 to 4½ in.), stems removed
- 1 lb. fresh asparagus, trimmed and cut into 2-in. pieces
- 10 oz. cherry tomatoes
  Optional: Grated Parmesan cheese and additional fresh minced oregano

DIRECTIONS

In a small bowl, combine the first 6 ingredients. Brush polenta with 2 Tbsp. oil mixture. Transfer to Crisper Tray. Slide the Crisper Tray into Shelf Position 4.

Brush mushrooms with 1 Tbsp. oil mixture; transfer to Grill Plate. Slide the Grill Plate into Shelf Position 6. Toss asparagus and tomatoes with the remaining oil mixture; transfer to Baking Pan. Slide the Pizza Rack into Shelf Position 1; place the Baking Pan on the Pizza Rack. Turn the Function Dial to Air Fry/Grill, set the temperature to 425° and set the timer to 30 minutes.

When there are 15 minutes left on the timer, flip the mushrooms and rotate the Baking Pan. Cook until vegetables are tender, 10-15 minutes. If desired, serve with Parmesan cheese and additional oregano.

1 MUSHROOM WITH ¾ CUP VEGETABLES AND 2 SLICES POLENTA *283 cal., 14g fat (2g sat. fat), 0 chol., 739mg sod., 34g carb. (8g sugars, 4g fiber), 6g pro.*

PREP 15 min.   **COOK** 25 min.   **SERVES** 4

Meaty Fact
Portobello stems are tough and woody. Discard them, or use well-rinsed and coarsely chopped stems in future broths.

Seafood "Boil" Supper

INGREDIENTS

- 1 lb. baby red potatoes, cut into quarters
- 1 tsp. olive oil
- 3 tsp. Old Bay seafood seasoning, divided
- 1 lb. fresh mussels, scrubbed and beards removed
- 1 lb. fresh clams, scrubbed
- 1 lb. uncooked shrimp (26-30 per lb.), peeled and deveined
- 12 oz. cod fillet
- 3 medium ears sweet corn, cut in half
- 7 oz. smoked sausage links, cut into 2-in. pieces
- Optional: Lemon wedges, clarified butter and minced fresh parsley

DIRECTIONS

Toss potatoes with oil and ½ tsp. Old Bay; transfer to Crisper Tray. Slide Grill Plate into Shelf Position 6. Slide the Crisper Tray into Shelf Position 4. Turn the Function Dial to Air Fry/Grill, set the temperature to 400° and set the timer to 15 minutes.

Season mussels, clams and shrimp with 2 tsp. Old Bay; season cod and corn with ½ tsp. Old Bay. When the 15-minute cycle ends, add seafood mixture to Crisper Tray on top of potatoes. Place cod, corn and sausage on the Grill Plate. Set timer for 15 minutes and cook until shrimp turn pink and cod flakes easily with a fork, 12-15 minutes. If desired, sprinkle with parsley and serve with lemon wedges and clarified butter.

1 SERVING *389 cal., 14g fat (5g sat. fat), 161mg chol., 1057mg sod., 27g carb. (5g sugars, 2g fiber), 40g pro.*

PREP 10 min.   **COOK** 30 min.   **SERVES** 6

AIR FRY **GRILL**

Smoked Sausage & Veggie Supper

INGREDIENTS

- 1 large sweet onion, halved and sliced
- 8 fresh Brussels sprouts, thinly sliced
- 1 medium tomato, chopped
- ½ cup sliced fresh mushrooms
- ½ cup Greek vinaigrette, divided
- 1 pkg. (13½ oz.) smoked sausage links, cut into ½-in. slices
- 1 small yellow summer squash, halved and sliced
- 1 small zucchini, halved and sliced
- 1 small sweet yellow pepper, sliced
- 1 small green pepper, sliced

DIRECTIONS

Slide the Grill Plate into Shelf Position 6 and slide the Pizza Rack into Shelf Position 4. Turn the Function Dial to Air Fry/Grill, set the temperature to 450° and set the timer to 30 minutes. Preheat the grill for 10 minutes.

Meanwhile, combine onion, Brussels sprouts, tomato, mushrooms and ¼ cup vinaigrette in a large bowl; toss to coat. Place mixture in the Baking Pan. In the same bowl, combine sausage, summer squash, zucchini, yellow and green peppers and remaining ¼ cup vinaigrette; toss to coat.

When there are 20 minutes left on the timer, place sausage mixture on the Grill Plate and place the Baking Pan on the Pizza Rack. Cook until vegetables are tender and sausage is lightly browned, stirring once.

2 CUPS *481 cal., 37g fat (13g sat. fat), 64mg chol., 1428mg sod., 20g carb. (12g sugars, 4g fiber), 17g pro.*

PREP 20 min.   **COOK** 20 min.   **SERVES** 4

HOW TO

Julienne Peppers Like a Pro

Trim the stem from the pepper so pepper sits flat on its top. Cut 1 side off the pepper, being careful to leave the seeds and core intact. Rotate pepper and cut off another side. Continue turning and cutting until only the core remains; trim or discard core. Cut each pepper fillet into thin strips.

Tandoori Chicken Dinner

INGREDIENTS

- 1 cup plain Greek yogurt
- 3 Tbsp. tandoori masala seasoning
- 1/8 to 1/4 tsp. crushed red pepper flakes, optional
- 8 boneless skinless chicken thighs (about 2 lbs.)
- 2 medium sweet potatoes, peeled and cut into 1/2-in. wedges
- 1 Tbsp. olive oil
- 16 cherry tomatoes
   Lemon slices
   Optional: Naan flatbreads and minced fresh cilantro

DIRECTIONS

In a large bowl, whisk yogurt, tandoori seasoning and, if desired, pepper flakes until blended. Add chicken and turn to coat. Cover and refrigerate 6-8 hours, turning occasionally.

Toss sweet potatoes with oil; place on the Crisper Tray. Slide the Crisper Tray into Shelf Position 4. Slide the Grill Plate into Shelf Position 6. Turn the Function Dial to Air Fry/Grill, set the temperature to 450° and set the timer to 20 minutes.

When there are 15 minutes left on the timer, add the tomatoes to the Crisper Tray.

Drain chicken, discarding marinade in bowl. When there are slightly more than 10 minutes left on the timer, place chicken and lemon slices on the Grill Plate. When there are 5 minutes left on the timer, flip the chicken and lemon slices, and continue to cook until a thermometer inserted into chicken reads 170°. If desired, serve with naan and cilantro.

1 SERVING *540 cal., 25g fat (8g sat. fat), 164mg chol., 168mg sod., 29g carb. (13g sugars, 6g fiber), 46g pro.*

PREP 15 min. + marinating   **COOK** 20 min.
SERVES 4

AIR FRY **BROIL**

Chicken Parmesan Dinner

INGREDIENTS

- 1 large egg
- 1 Tbsp. water
- ½ cup panko bread crumbs
- ½ cup grated Parmesan cheese
- ¾ tsp. salt, divided
- 1 tsp. pepper
- 1 tsp. garlic powder
- 4 boneless skinless chicken breast halves (6 oz. each)
  Olive oil-flavored cooking spray
- 4 cups fresh or frozen broccoli florets (about 10 oz.)
- 1 cup marinara sauce
- 1 cup shredded mozzarella cheese
- ¼ cup minced fresh basil, optional

DIRECTIONS

Lightly coat Baking Pan with cooking spray. In a shallow bowl, whisk egg with water. In a separate shallow bowl, stir together panko, cheese, ½ tsp. salt, pepper and garlic powder. Dip 1 chicken breast in egg; allow excess to drip off. Then dip in crumb mixture, patting to help coating adhere. Repeat with remaining chicken. Place chicken breasts in Baking Pan. Spritz with cooking spray.

Slide the Pizza Rack into Shelf Position 2. Place the Baking Pan on the Pizza Rack. Turn the Function Dial to Air Fry, set the temperature to 400° and set the timer to 10 minutes. Meanwhile, spread broccoli in a single layer in Crisper Tray. Spritz with cooking spray; sprinkle with remaining ¼ tsp. salt (if broccoli is frozen, break pieces apart). When the timed cycle ends, slide Crisper Tray into Shelf Position 5. Set timer for 10 minutes longer. When cycle ends, remove pan from oven.

Spread marinara sauce over chicken; top with shredded cheese. Return Baking Pan to Pizza Rack. Turn Function Dial to Broil, set temperature to 450° and set timer to 10 minutes. Broil until cheese is golden brown and broccoli is tender, 5-7 minutes. Top with basil if desired.

1 SERVING *399 cal., 16g fat (7g sat. fat), 145mg chol., 1154mg sod., 15g carb. (5g sugars, 3g fiber), 48g pro.*

| **PREP** 15 min. | **COOK** 25 min. | **SERVES** 4 |

Say Cheese
A quick spritz of cooking spray will keep cheese from sticking to the grater. Plus, cleanup will be a lot easier.

Turkey Tenderloin & Root Veggie Supper

INGREDIENTS

- 4 medium carrots, peeled and cut into ½-in. pieces
- 2 medium parsnips, peeled and cut into ½-in. pieces
- 2 medium onions, cut into ½-in. pieces
- 2 tsp. canola oil
- ½ tsp. salt
- ¼ tsp. pepper
- 6 bacon strips
- 1 pkg. (24 oz.) rotisserie-flavored turkey breast tenderloins
   Minced fresh parsley, optional

DIRECTIONS

Slide the Grill Plate into Shelf Position 6. Turn the Function Dial to Air Fry/Grill, set the temperature to 400° and set timer for 35 minutes. Preheat the grill for 5 minutes.

Meanwhile, in a large bowl, toss carrots, parsnips and onions with oil; sprinkle with salt and pepper. Place vegetables on the Crisper Tray; lay bacon slices over vegetables. When there are 30 minutes left on the timer, slide the Crisper Tray into Shelf Position 4 and place tenderloins on the Grill Plate.

Cook until a thermometer inserted in turkey reads 165° and vegetables are tender, 25-30 minutes. Chop bacon; stir into vegetable mixture. If desired, sprinkle with parsley.

1 SERVING *310 cal., 14g fat (4g sat. fat), 58mg chol., 997mg sod., 20g carb. (7g sugars, 4g fiber), 28g pro.*

PREP 15 min.	COOK 30 min.	SERVES 6

Carrot Tip

Don't peel carrots in recipes like this—the skin contains lots of nutrients. But do scrub them well before chopping.

Rotisserie Magic

Flavor Faves

TAKE ANY OF THE RECIPES IN THIS CHAPTER
BEYOND THE BASICS BY MIXING UP A RUB OR
GLAZE TO ADD DISTINCT FLAVOR AND APPEAL.

1. HONEY GLAZE

Stir together 1 cup
honey, ½ cup **brown
sugar**, 1 tsp. **ground
cloves** and ½ tsp.
ground mustard.

2. HOISIN GLAZE

Stir together 2 Tbsp.
Dijon mustard, 2 Tbsp.
hoisin sauce, 2 Tbsp.
oyster sauce, 2 Tbsp.
honey, 2 tsp. **reduced-
sodium soy sauce** and
1 tsp. **minced fresh
gingerroot**.

3. JAVA-SPICE RUB

Combine 1 Tbsp. **finely
ground coffee**, 1 tsp.
kosher salt, 1 tsp. **brown
sugar**, 1 tsp. **chili
powder**, ½ tsp. **ground
cumin**, ½ tsp. **ground
cinnamon**, ½ tsp. **pepper**
and ¼ tsp. **garlic powder**.
Store in an airtight
container.

4. MAPLE GLAZE

Stir together 2 Tbsp.
maple syrup, 2 Tbsp.
hoisin sauce and 2 tsp.
prepared mustard.

5. PEACH GLAZE

Stir together ¼ cup
peach preserves, 2 Tbsp.
chicken broth or water,
1 Tbsp. **balsamic vinegar**,
2 tsp. **minced fresh
cilantro**, ¾ tsp. **ground
ancho chile pepper** and
1 minced garlic clove.

6. HORSERADISH GLAZE

Stir together 1 cup **brown
sugar**, 1/3 cup **prepared
horseradish** and ¼ cup
lemon juice.

7. SOUTHWESTERN
SEASONING MIX

Combine ¼ cup **chili
powder**, ¼ cup **onion
powder**, 2 Tbsp. **ground
cumin**, 2 Tbsp. **ground
coriander**, 2 Tbsp. **dried
oregano**, 2 Tbsp. **dried
basil**, 1 Tbsp. **dried
thyme** and 1 Tbsp. **garlic
powder**. Store in an
airtight container.

8. BOURBON GLAZE
Stir together 1 cup **brown sugar**, ⅓ cup **bourbon**, 1 Tbsp. **orange marmalade**, 2 tsp. **ground mustard** and ⅛ tsp. **ground coriander**.

9. ALL-AMERICAN RUB
Stir together ½ cup **brown sugar**, 2 Tbsp. **dried minced onion**, 1 Tbsp. **garlic powder**, 1 Tbsp. **ground mustard**, ½ tsp. **cayenne pepper** and ⅛ tsp. **ground nutmeg**. Store in an airtight container.

10. CAJUN SEASONING
Combine 1 Tbsp. **onion powder**, 1 Tbsp. **white pepper**, 1 Tbsp. **garlic powder**, 1 Tbsp. **ground mustard**, 1 Tbsp. **paprika**, 1½ tsp. **celery seed** and 1½ tsp. **dried thyme**. Store in an airtight container.

11. CITRUS APRICOT GLAZE
Stir together ⅓ cup **apricot preserves**, 3 Tbsp. melted **butter**, ½ tsp. grated **orange zest**, ½ tsp. **lemon juice**, ¼ tsp. **salt** and ¼ tsp. **ground nutmeg**.

12. PINEAPPLE GLAZE
Stir together 1 can (8 oz.) **unsweetened crushed pineapple** (drained), ½ cup **apricot jam**, 1 Tbsp. **spicy brown mustard** and 2 tsp. **prepared horseradish**.

13. RASPBERRY CHIPOTLE GLAZE
Mix 1 jar (12 oz.) **seedless raspberry jam**, 2 Tbsp. **white vinegar**, 2 **chipotle peppers in adobo sauce** (drained, seeded and minced), 3 minced **garlic cloves** and 2 tsp. **coarsely ground pepper**.

14. MOLASSES BBQ GLAZE
Stir together ¼ cup **ketchup**, ¼ cup **honey**, ¼ cup **molasses**, 1 Tbsp. **prepared mustard**, ½ tsp. **cayenne pepper** and ½ tsp. **salt**.

15. GREEK SEASONING
Combine 1½ tsp. **dried oregano**, 1 tsp. **dried mint**, 1 tsp. **dried thyme**, ½ tsp. **dried basil**, ½ tsp. **dried marjoram**, ½ tsp. **dried minced onion** and ¼ tsp. **dried minced garlic**. Store in an airtight container.

Rotisserie Chicken

INGREDIENTS

- 2 Tbsp. olive oil
- 1 broiler/fryer chicken (3 to 4 lbs.)
- 2 tsp. kosher salt
- 1 tsp. pepper

DIRECTIONS

Rub oil over chicken and sprinkle with salt and pepper. Attach 1 of the Rotisserie Forks to the Rotisserie Spit and tighten the screws on the Fork. Slide the chicken onto the Spit and into the secured Fork. Secure the chicken on the Spit with the other Fork and screws. Tuck wings under chicken; tie drumsticks together. Insert the Spit into the Rotisserie connections.

Turn the Function Dial to Rotisserie, set temperature to 350° and set the timer to 90 minutes. Cook until the internal temperature reaches 170°-175° in the thickest part of a thigh, 80-90 minutes. Remove chicken and Spit from unit and let stand for 10 minutes. Remove chicken from Spit; carve chicken.

1 SERVING *296 cal., 16g fat (3g sat. fat), 110mg chol., 1053mg sod., 0 carb. (0 sugars, 0 fiber), 36g pro.*

PREP 10 min.   **COOK** 1 hour 20 min. + standing
SERVES 4

Take the Heat

When the Rotisserie cooking cycle is complete, use silicone oven mitts (or potholders) to help remove food on the Spit from the PowerXL Air Fryer Grill. Silicone provides the best protection and flexibility. Plus, it's super easy to clean!

Rotisserie Cornish Hens

INGREDIENTS

- 2 Tbsp. olive oil
- 2 Cornish game hens (20 to 24 oz. each)
- 2 tsp. kosher salt
- 1 tsp. pepper

DIRECTIONS

Rub oil over hens and sprinkle with salt and pepper. Attach 1 of the Rotisserie Forks to the Rotisserie Spit and tighten the screws on the Fork. Slide 1 hen onto the Spit and into the secured Fork. Slide the second hen onto the Spit and secure on the Spit with the other Fork and screws. Tuck wings under the hens; tie the drumsticks together. Insert the Spit into the Rotisserie connections.

Turn the Function Dial to Rotisserie, set temperature to 350° and set the timer to 90 minutes. Cook until the internal temperature reaches 170°-175° in the thickest part of a thigh, 80-90 minutes. Remove Spit from unit and let hens stand for 10 minutes. Remove hens from Spit; cut hens in half to serve.

½ HEN *235 cal., 19g fat (4g sat. fat), 88mg chol., 1003mg sod., 0 carb. (0 sugars, 0 fiber), 15g pro.*

PREP 10 min.   **COOK** 1 hour 20 min. + standing
SERVES 4

Truss Up

Trussing, or tying up, a chicken for rotisserie cooking prevents the legs (and wings) from hitting the heating element as the bird rotates on the spit. It also lifts the legs, exposing more of the bird's skin to the hot oven air. The extra support gives the chicken a more uniform shape, which helps it cook more evenly. And all of that contributes to getting deliciously crispy skin.

Rotisserie Eye of Round Roast

INGREDIENTS

- 2 Tbsp. olive oil
- 1 beef eye round roast (2½ lbs.)
- 2 tsp. kosher salt
- 1 tsp. pepper

DIRECTIONS

Rub oil over roast and sprinkle with salt and pepper. Attach 1 of the Rotisserie Forks to the Rotisserie Spit and tighten the screws on the Fork. Slide the roast onto the Spit and into the secured Fork. Secure the roast on the Spit with the other Fork and screws. Insert the Spit into the Rotisserie connections.

Turn the Function Dial to Rotisserie, set temperature to 350° and set the timer to 60 minutes. Cook until meat reaches desired doneness (for medium-rare, a thermometer should read 135°; medium, 140°; medium-well, 145°), 55-60 minutes. Remove roast and Spit from unit and let stand for 10 minutes before removing roast from Spit. Let stand an additional 10 minutes before slicing.

5 OZ. COOKED BEEF *202 cal., 8g fat (2g sat. fat), 58mg chol., 520mg sod., 0 carb. (0 sugars, 0 fiber), 31g pro.*

PREP 10 min. **COOK** 55 min. + standing **SERVES** 8

Rotisserie Ham

INGREDIENTS

1 fully cooked boneless ham (5 to 7 lbs.)
1 to 2 cups Bourbon Glaze (page 93), optional

DIRECTIONS

Using a sharp knife, score surface of the ham with ¼-in.-deep cuts in a diamond pattern. Attach 1 of the Rotisserie Forks to the Rotisserie Spit and tighten the screws on the Fork. Slide the ham onto the Spit and into the secured Fork. Secure the ham on the Spit with the other Fork and screws. Insert the Spit into the Rotisserie connections.

Turn the Function Dial to Rotisserie, set temperature to 325° and set the timer to 60 minutes. Cook until the internal temperature reaches 140°, 50-60 minutes, brushing with glaze the last 30 minutes if desired. Remove Spit from unit and let ham stand 10 minutes. Remove ham from Spit; carve ham.

4 OZ. HAM *150 cal., 5g fat (2g sat. fat), 72mg chol., 1471mg sod., 0 carb. (0 sugars, 0 fiber), 26g pro.*

PREP 10 min. **COOK** 50 min. + standing **SERVES** 16

Rotisserie Pineapple

INGREDIENTS

1   fresh pineapple, peeled
¼   cup Bourbon Glaze (page 93)

DIRECTIONS

Insert Rotisserie Spit through center of pineapple lengthwise; slide the forks onto each side of the Spit and secure them in place by tightening the screws. Baste the pineapple with some of the Bourbon Glaze. Insert the Spit into the Rotisserie connections.

Turn the Function Dial to Rotisserie, set temperature to 425° and set timer to 10 minutes. When timed cycle ends, baste pineapple with more glaze; set timer for 5 minutes. Repeat until the pineapple is well glazed and reaches 160°. Remove Spit from unit; remove pineapple from Spit. Cut pineapple into 6 pieces.

1 PIECE *112 cal., 0 fat (0 sat. fat), 0 chol., 4mg sod., 28 carb. (22 sugars, 2 fiber), 1g pro.*

PREP 10 min.   **COOK** 15 min.   **SERVES** 6

 WHO KNEW? **Sweet!**
Rotisserie pineapple is definitely good enough to eat on its own, but we've offered a slew of ways to serve up this tangy treat in the Tasty Surprises chapter. Check out "Tropical Zing" on page 218.

Rotisserie Pork Loin

INGREDIENTS

- 2 Tbsp. olive oil
- 1 boneless pork loin roast (3 lbs.)
- 2 tsp. kosher salt
- 1 tsp. pepper

DIRECTIONS

Rub oil over pork loin and sprinkle with salt and pepper. Attach 1 of the Rotisserie Forks to the Rotisserie Spit and tighten the screws on the Fork. Slide the pork loin onto the Spit and into the secured Fork. Secure the pork on the Spit with the other Fork and screws. Insert the Spit into the Rotisserie connections.

Turn the Function Dial to Rotisserie, set temperature to 400° and set the timer to 60 minutes. Cook until the internal temperature reaches 140°, 50-60 minutes. Remove Spit from unit and let pork stand 10 minutes. Remove pork from Spit; let pork stand 10 minutes longer before carving.

6 OZ. COOKED PORK *242 cal., 11g fat (3g sat. fat), 85mg chol., 529mg sod., 0 carb. (0 sugars, 0 fiber), 33g pro.*

PREP 15 min.   **COOK** 50 min. + standing   **SERVES** 8

Rotisserie Roast Beef

INGREDIENTS

- 1 beef rump roast (3 lbs.) or bottom round roast
- 2 Tbsp. olive oil
- 2 tsp. kosher salt
- 1 tsp. pepper

DIRECTIONS

Attach 1 of the Rotisserie Forks to the Rotisserie Spit and tighten the screws on the Fork. Slide the roast onto the Spit and into the secured Fork. Secure the roast on the Spit with the other Fork and screws. Brush roast with oil; sprinkle with salt and pepper. Insert the Spit into the Rotisserie connections.

Turn the Function Dial to Rotisserie, set temperature to 400° and set the timer to 10 minutes. When 10-minute cycle ends, set the temperature to 325° and set the timer to 40 minutes. Cook until meat reaches desired doneness (for medium-rare, a thermometer should read 135°; medium, 140°; medium-well, 145°), 35-40 minutes. Remove Spit and roast from unit; let roast stand 10 minutes. Remove roast from Spit and let roast stand 10 minutes longer before slicing.

5 OZ. COOKED BEEF *245 cal., 11g fat (3g sat. fat), 101mg chol., 534mg sod., 0 carb. (0 sugars, 0 fiber), 33g pro.*

PREP 10 min.   **COOK** 45 min. + standing   **SERVES** 8

PRO TIP!

Tie It Up

For even cooking with larger cuts of meat, tie the roast firmly with butcher's twine. When the size and shape of the meat is consistent, you'll get even temperatures throughout. And it will look nicer!

For Meat & Seafood Lovers

Air-Fryer Steak Fajitas

INGREDIENTS

- 2 large tomatoes, seeded and chopped
- ½ cup diced red onion
- ¼ cup lime juice
- 1 jalapeno pepper, seeded and minced
- 3 Tbsp. minced fresh cilantro
- 2 tsp. ground cumin, divided
- ¾ tsp. salt, divided
- 1 beef flank steak (about 1½ lbs.)
- 1 large onion, halved and sliced
- 6 whole wheat tortillas (8 in.), warmed
  Optional: Avocado slices and lime wedges

DIRECTIONS

For salsa, place first 5 ingredients in a small bowl; stir in 1 tsp. cumin and ¼ tsp. salt. Let stand until serving.

Sprinkle steak with the remaining cumin and salt. Slide the Pizza Rack into Shelf Position 4. Turn the Function Dial to Air Fry, set the temperature to 400° and set the timer to 20 minutes. Place steak on greased Baking Pan; slide pan onto Pizza Rack. Cook until meat reaches desired doneness (for medium-rare, a thermometer should read 135°; medium, 140°; medium-well, 145°), 6-8 minutes per side. Remove and let stand 5 minutes.

Meanwhile, place onion on Crisper Tray. Slide the Crisper Tray into Shelf Position 4. Turn the Function Dial to Air Fry, set the temperature to 400° and set the timer to 5 minutes. Cook until crisp-tender, 2-3 minutes, stirring once.

Slice steak thinly across the grain; serve in tortillas with onion and salsa. If desired, serve with avocado slices and lime wedges.

1 FAJITA *309 cal., 9g fat (4g sat. fat), 54mg chol., 498mg sod., 29g carb. (3g sugars, 5g fiber), 27g pro.*

TAKES 30 min.   **SERVES** 6

Chicken with Peach-Avocado Salsa

INGREDIENTS

- 1 medium peach, peeled and chopped
- 1 medium ripe avocado, peeled and cubed
- ½ cup chopped sweet red pepper
- 3 Tbsp. finely chopped red onion
- 1 Tbsp. minced fresh basil
- 1 Tbsp. lime juice
- 1 tsp. hot pepper sauce
- ½ tsp. grated lime zest
- ¾ tsp. salt, divided
- ½ tsp. pepper, divided
- 4 boneless skinless chicken breast halves (6 oz. each)

DIRECTIONS

For salsa, in a small bowl, combine peach, avocado, red pepper, onion, basil, lime juice, hot sauce, lime zest, ¼ tsp. salt and ¼ tsp. pepper.

Slide the Grill Plate into Shelf Position 6. Turn the Function Dial to Grill, set the temperature to 350° and set the timer to 25 minutes. Let the grill preheat for 10 minutes. Meanwhile, sprinkle chicken with remaining salt and pepper.

When the grill has preheated, place chicken on Grill Plate. Grill 5 minutes. Turn; grill until a thermometer reads 165°, 7-9 minutes longer. Serve with salsa.

1 CHICKEN BREAST HALF WITH ½ CUP SALSA *265 cal., 9g fat (2g sat. fat), 94mg chol., 536mg sod., 9g carb. (4g sugars, 3g fiber), 36g pro.*

TAKES 30 min.   **SERVES** 4

Cilantro-Lime Shrimp

INGREDIENTS

- ⅓ cup chopped fresh cilantro
- 1½ tsp. grated lime zest
- ⅓ cup lime juice
- 1 jalapeno pepper, seeded and minced
- 2 Tbsp. olive oil
- 3 garlic cloves, minced
- ¼ tsp. salt
- ¼ tsp. ground cumin
- ¼ tsp. pepper
- 1 lb. uncooked shrimp (16-20 per lb.), peeled and deveined
- Lime wedges

DIRECTIONS

Mix the first 9 ingredients; toss with shrimp. Let stand 15 minutes.

Slide the Grill Plate into Shelf Position 6. Turn the Function Dial to Grill, set the temperature to 350° and set the timer to 20 minutes. Let the grill preheat for 10 minutes.

Thread shrimp and lime wedges onto 4 metal or soaked wooden skewers. When the grill has preheated, place shrimp on the Grill Plate. Grill until shrimp turn pink, 2-4 minutes per side.

1 KABOB *167 cal., 8g fat (1g sat. fat), 138mg chol., 284mg sod., 4g carb. (1g sugars, 0 fiber), 19g pro.*

TAKES 30 min.   **SERVES** 4

Save Time & Money

If you prefer to not mess with peeling and deveining fresh shrimp, pick up a bag of the frozen variety. It's cheaper, and frozen shrimp will keep for at least 3 months.

Ginger-Glazed Grilled Salmon

INGREDIENTS

- 2 Tbsp. reduced-sodium soy sauce
- 2 Tbsp. maple syrup
- 2 tsp. minced fresh gingerroot
- 2 garlic cloves, minced
- 4 salmon fillets (6 oz. each)

DIRECTIONS

Slide the Grill Plate into Shelf Position 6. Turn the Function Dial to Grill, set the temperature to 350° and set the timer to 20 minutes. Let the grill preheat for 10 minutes. Meanwhile, for glaze, mix the first 4 ingredients.

When the grill has preheated, place the salmon on the Grill Plate. Grill until fish just begins to flake easily with a fork, 4-5 minutes per side; brush top with half of the glaze after turning. Brush with the remaining glaze before serving.

1 FILLET *299 cal., 16g fat (3g sat. fat), 85mg chol., 374mg sod., 8g carb. (6g sugars, 0 fiber), 29g pro.*

TAKES 15 min.   **SERVES** 4

Grilled Dijon Pork Roast

INGREDIENTS

- ⅓ cup balsamic vinegar
- 3 Tbsp. Dijon mustard
- 1 Tbsp. honey
- 1 tsp. salt
- 1 boneless pork loin roast (3 to 4 lbs.)

DIRECTIONS

In a large bowl or shallow dish, whisk vinegar, mustard, honey and salt. Add pork and turn to coat. Cover and refrigerate at least 8 hours or overnight.

Slide the Grill Plate into Shelf Position 6. Turn the Function Dial to Grill, set the temperature to 325° and set the timer to 85 minutes. Let the grill preheat for 10 minutes.

Drain pork, discarding marinade. When the grill has preheated, place pork on the Grill Plate. Cook until a thermometer inserted in pork reads 145°, 60-75 minutes, turning occasionally. Let stand for 10 minutes before slicing.

3 OZ. COOKED PORK *149 cal., 5g fat (2g sat. fat), 56mg chol., 213mg sod., 2g carb. (1g sugars, 0 fiber), 22g pro.*

PREP 10 min. + marinating   **GRILL** 1 hour + standing
SERVES 12

Size Matters

Cooking smaller roasts and cuts of meat (2 lbs. or less) works best when trying to get the same temperature throughout. If the people that you're cooking for prefer different temperatures (i.e., one likes rare; another likes medium), a larger roast may work better. With 3-lb. and larger cuts, the ends will be more well done than the center.

Grilled Huli Huli Turkey Drumsticks

INGREDIENTS

- ⅔ cup packed brown sugar
- ½ cup ketchup
- ½ cup reduced-sodium soy sauce
- ¼ cup sherry or chicken broth
- 2 tsp. minced fresh gingerroot
- 2 tsp. minced garlic
- 4 turkey drumsticks (1½ lbs. each)
  Green onions, chopped

DIRECTIONS

Mix the first 6 ingredients. Reserve ¾ cup for basting; cover and refrigerate. Pour remaining marinade into a large baking dish. Add drumsticks and turn to coat. Cover and refrigerate 8 hours or overnight.

Slide the Grill Plate into Shelf Position 6. Turn the Function Dial to Grill, set the temperature to 325° and set the timer to 50 minutes. Let the grill preheat for 10 minutes. Drain turkey, discarding marinade.

When the grill has preheated, place the turkey on the Grill Plate. Cook until a thermometer reads 175°, 40-45 minutes. Turn the drumsticks occasionally throughout cooking. Baste often with reserved marinade during the last 10 minutes. Let stand 15 minutes; garnish with green onions.

8 OZ. COOKED TURKEY *486 cal., 20g fat (6g sat. fat), 171mg chol., 671mg sod., 16g carb. (15g sugars, 0 fiber), 57g pro.*

PREP 15 min. + marinating
GRILL 40 min. + standing   **SERVES** 8

HOW TO

Quickly Separate and Peel Garlic Cloves

Place the head of garlic in a bowl and smash it with the bottom of another bowl. You can also smash it between 2 cutting boards. Next, put the whole crushed bulb in a hard-sided bowl with a similarly sized bowl over the top. Metal is best, but you can use glass or even a firm plastic food storage container with a lid. Shake vigorously for 10-15 seconds to separate the papery outer layer from all the garlic cloves. Discard the skins and start mincing.

Grilled Ribeye with Garlic Blue Cheese Mustard

INGREDIENTS

- 1 cup half-and-half cream
- ½ cup Dijon mustard
- ¼ cup plus 2 tsp. crumbled blue cheese, divided
- 1 garlic clove, minced
- 2 beef ribeye steaks (1½ in. thick and 12 oz. each)
- 1 Tbsp. olive oil
- ¼ tsp. salt
- ¼ tsp. pepper

DIRECTIONS

Slide the Grill Plate into Shelf Position 6. Turn the Function Dial to Grill, set the temperature to 400° and set the timer to 25 minutes. Let the grill preheat for 10 minutes.

Meanwhile, in a small saucepan over medium heat, whisk together cream, mustard, ¼ cup blue cheese and garlic. Bring to a simmer. Reduce heat to low; whisk occasionally.

Rub meat with olive oil; sprinkle with salt and pepper. When the grill has preheated, place steaks on the Grill Plate. Grill steaks until meat reaches desired doneness (for medium-rare, a thermometer should read 135°; medium, 140°; medium-well, 145°), 4-6 minutes on each side. Remove from grill; let stand 10 minutes while sauce finishes cooking. When sauce is reduced by half, pour over steaks; top with the remaining 2 tsp. blue cheese.

½ **STEAK WITH 3 TBSP. SAUCE** *547 cal., 39g fat (17g sat. fat), 138mg chol., 1088mg sod., 3g carb. (2g sugars, 0 fiber), 34g pro.*

PREP 20 min.　　**GRILL** 10 min. + standing　　**SERVES** 4

WHO KNEW? **Smell Fresh**

To remove the smell of garlic from your hands, scrub them with a mixture of baking soda and salt, then rinse with warm water. Alternatively, you can wash your hands with soap and water, and then rub them over a stainless steel surface (such as the sink faucet, an appliance or a pot).

Whiskey Pineapple Chicken

INGREDIENTS

- 1 cup bourbon
- 1 cup unsweetened pineapple juice
- ½ cup hoisin sauce
- 1 Tbsp. minced fresh gingerroot
- 3 tsp. coarsely ground pepper, divided
- 2 tsp. Worcestershire sauce
- 4 garlic cloves, minced
- 1½ tsp. kosher salt, divided
- 2½ lbs. boneless skinless chicken thighs
- ½ cup sliced sweet red pepper
- ½ cup sliced yellow onion
- 1 Tbsp. olive oil

DIRECTIONS

Whisk together the bourbon, pineapple juice, hoisin sauce, ginger, 1½ tsp. pepper, Worcestershire sauce, garlic and ½ tsp. salt until blended. Place chicken in a shallow dish. Add half the marinade; turn to coat. Cover and refrigerate, overnight, turning occasionally. Cover and refrigerate remaining marinade.

Slide the Grill Plate into Shelf Position 6. Turn the Function Dial to Grill, set the temperature to 375° and set the timer to 25 minutes. Let the grill preheat for 10 minutes. Drain chicken, discarding marinade. Toss red pepper and onion slices in oil and remaining salt and pepper; set aside.

When grill has preheated, place the chicken on the Grill Plate. Cook until a thermometer reads 170°, 5-6 minutes on each side. Remove and let rest. Grill pepper and onion, turning frequently, until soft, 5-7 minutes. Meanwhile, in a small saucepan over medium heat on a stovetop, cook the reserved marinade until slightly thickened, stirring occasionally, about 10 minutes. Chop grilled pepper and onion. Sprinkle over chicken; serve with sauce.

1 SERVING *439 cal., 20g fat (5g sat. fat), 152mg chol., 735mg sod., 13g carb. (8g sugars, 1g fiber), 43g pro.*

PREP 20 min. + marinating   **GRILL** 15 min.

SERVES 5

Italian Crumb-Crusted Beef Roast

INGREDIENTS

1	beef sirloin tip roast (3 lbs.)
¼	tsp. salt
¾	cup Italian-style panko bread crumbs
¼	cup mayonnaise
3	Tbsp. dried minced onion
½	tsp. Italian seasoning
¼	tsp. pepper

DIRECTIONS

Place roast on Baking Pan; sprinkle with salt. In a small bowl, mix the remaining ingredients; press onto top and sides of roast.

Slide the Pizza Rack into Shelf Position 5. Place the Baking Pan on the Pizza Rack. Turn the Function Dial to Pizza/Bake, set the temperature to 325° and set the timer to 120 minutes. Roast until meat reaches desired doneness (for medium-rare, a thermometer should read 135°; medium, 140°; medium well, 145°), 1¾-2¼ hours, adding additional time to unit as needed. Remove roast; tent with foil. Let stand for 10 minutes before slicing.

5 OZ. COOKED BEEF *319 cal., 15g fat (3g sat. fat), 111mg chol., 311mg sod., 7g carb. (0 sugars, 0 fiber), 35g pro.*

PREP 10 min.   **BAKE** 1¾ hours + standing
SERVES 8

Spice-Brined Turkey

INGREDIENTS

2 qt. water
1 cup paprika
1 cup chili powder
2 pkg. (3 oz. each) crab boil in a bag
½ cup packed brown sugar
2 medium onions, quartered, divided
2 Tbsp. dried rosemary, crushed
2 Tbsp. dried thyme
10 garlic cloves, peeled and halved, divided
2 qt. cold water
2 turkey-size oven roasting bags
1 turkey (10 to 12 lbs.)
¼ cup olive oil

RUB
3 Tbsp. paprika
3 Tbsp. chili powder
2 Tbsp. garlic powder
2 Tbsp. ground cumin

DIRECTIONS

In a stockpot, combine water, paprika, chili powder, crab boil in bag, brown sugar, 4 onion quarters, rosemary, thyme and half of the garlic. Bring to a boil. Cook and stir 5 minutes. Remove from heat. Add cold water to cool the brine to room temperature.

Place 1 oven roasting bag inside the other. Place turkey inside both bags; pour in cooled brine. Seal bags, pressing out as much air as possible; turn to coat turkey. Place in a shallow roasting pan. Refrigerate 18-24 hours, turning occasionally.

Remove turkey from brine, discarding brine in bag; rinse turkey and pat dry. Place turkey on the Baking Pan. Place remaining onion and garlic in turkey cavity. Drizzle oil over turkey. Mix rub ingredients; rub over the skin.

Slide the Pizza Rack into Shelf Position 6. Place the Baking Pan on the Pizza Rack. Turn the Function Dial to Grill, set the temperature to 350° and set the timer to 120 minutes. Cook until a thermometer inserted in thickest part of thigh reads 170-175°, 1¾-2¼ hours, adding additional time to unit as needed. Remove; cover and let stand 20 minutes before carving.

8 OZ. COOKED TURKEY *728 cal., 34g fat (9g sat. fat), 246mg chol., 632mg sod., 31g carb. (14g sugars, 11g fiber), 77g pro.*

PREP 30 min. + brining
COOK 1¾ hours + standing   **SERVES** 10

Spinach Tomato Burgers

INGREDIENTS

- 1 large egg, lightly beaten
- 2 Tbsp. fat-free milk
- ½ cup soft bread crumbs
- 1 tsp. dried basil
- ½ tsp. salt
- ¼ tsp. pepper
- 1 lb. lean ground beef (90% lean)
- 4 whole wheat hamburger buns, split
- ¼ cup spinach dip
- ¼ cup julienned soft sun-dried tomatoes (not packed in oil)
  Lettuce leaves

DIRECTIONS

Slide the Grill Plate into Shelf Position 6. Turn the Function Dial to Grill, set the temperature to 350° and set the timer to 20 minutes. Let the grill preheat for 10 minutes.

Combine the first 6 ingredients. Add beef; mix lightly but thoroughly. Shape into four ½-in.-thick patties.

When the grill has preheated, place burgers on the Grill Plate. Cook until a thermometer reads 160°, 4-5 minutes per side. Grill buns, cut side down, until toasted. Serve burgers on buns; top with spinach dip, tomatoes and lettuce.

1 BURGER *389 cal., 17g fat (6g sat. fat), 125mg chol., 737mg sod., 29g carb. (7g sugars, 4g fiber), 29g pro.*

TAKES 20 min.   **SERVES** 4

HOW TO

Make Your Own Ground Beef
Freeze 1 lb. chuck roast for 15 minutes. Cut the frozen meat into small cubes; place the cubes in a food processor. Pulse 20 to 22 times until the meat is coarsely ground.

Ultimate Grilled Pork Chops

INGREDIENTS

- ¼ cup kosher salt
- ¼ cup sugar
- 2 cups water
- 2 cups ice water
- 4 center-cut pork rib chops (1 in. thick and 8 oz. each)
- 2 Tbsp. canola oil

BASIC RUB
- 3 Tbsp. paprika
- 1 tsp. each garlic powder, onion powder, ground cumin and ground mustard
- 1 tsp. coarsely ground pepper
- ½ tsp. ground chipotle pepper

DIRECTIONS

In a large saucepan, combine salt, sugar and 2 cups water; cook and stir over medium heat until salt and sugar are dissolved. Remove from heat. Add 2 cups ice water to cool brine to room temperature.

Place pork chops in a large resealable plastic bag; add cooled brine. Seal bag, pressing out as much air as possible; turn to coat chops. Place in a 13x9-in. baking dish. Refrigerate 8-12 hours.

Remove chops from brine; rinse and pat dry. Discard brine. Brush both sides of chops with oil. In a small bowl, mix rub ingredients; rub over pork chops. Let stand at room temperature 30 minutes.

Slide the Grill Plate into Shelf Position 6. Turn the Function Dial to Grill, set the temperature to 350° and set the timer to 25 minutes. Let the grill preheat for 10 minutes. When the grill has preheated, place the chops on the Grill Plate. Cook until a thermometer reads 145°, 4-6 minutes on each side. Let stand for 5 minutes before serving.

1 PORK CHOP *300 cal., 18g fat (4g sat. fat), 72mg chol., 130mg sod., 5g carb. (1g sugars, 2g fiber), 30g pro.*

PREP 20 min. + brining   **GRILL** 10 min.   **SERVES** 4

Faster Cooking
Larger cuts of meats and veggies will take longer to cook through. To speed things up, cut smaller slices or cubes.

Sensational Sides

Air-Fryer Roasted Green Beans

INGREDIENTS

1 lb. fresh green beans, cut into 2-in. pieces
½ lb. sliced fresh mushrooms
1 small red onion, halved and thinly sliced
2 Tbsp. olive oil
1 tsp. Italian seasoning
¼ tsp. salt
⅛ tsp. pepper

DIRECTIONS

In a large bowl, combine all ingredients; toss to coat.

Arrange vegetables on greased Crisper Tray. Slide the Crisper Tray into Shelf Position 4. Turn the Function Dial to Air Fry, set the temperature to 375° and set timer to 20 minutes. Cook until vegetables are just tender, 8-10 minutes. Stir to redistribute; cook until browned, 8-10 minutes longer.

⅔ CUP *76 cal., 5g fat (1g sat. fat), 0 chol., 105mg sod., 8g carb. (3g sugars, 3g fiber), 3g pro.*

PREP 15 min.   **COOK** 20 min.   **SERVES** 6

Jalapeno Popper Mexican Street Corn

INGREDIENTS

- 4 ears fresh sweet corn, husked
- 2 jalapeno peppers
- 3 Tbsp. canola oil, divided
- ¾ tsp. salt, divided
- ¼ cup panko bread crumbs
- ½ tsp. smoked paprika
- ½ tsp. dried Mexican oregano
- 4 oz. cream cheese, softened
- ¼ cup media crema table cream or sour cream thinned with 1 tsp. 2% milk
- 2 Tbsp. lime juice
  Ground chipotle pepper or chili powder
  Chopped fresh cilantro, optional

DIRECTIONS

Slide the Grill Plate into Shelf Position 6. Turn the Function Dial to Air Fry/Grill, set the temperature to 425° and set timer to 25 minutes. Let grill preheat for 10 minutes. Meanwhile, rub corn and jalapenos with 2 Tbsp. canola oil. When the grill has preheated, place corn and jalapenos on the Grill Plate. Cook until lightly charred on all sides, 10-12 minutes. When jalapenos are cool enough to handle, remove skin, seeds and membranes; chop finely. Set aside.

Sprinkle corn with ½ tsp. salt. In a small skillet, heat remaining oil over medium heat. Add panko; cook and stir until starting to brown. Add paprika and oregano; cook until crumbs are toasted and fragrant.

Meanwhile, combine cream cheese, crema, lime juice and remaining salt; spread over corn. Sprinkle with bread crumbs, jalapenos, chipotle pepper and, if desired, cilantro.

1 EAR OF CORN *339 cal., 26g fat (9g sat. fat), 39mg chol., 568mg sod., 25g carb. (8g sugars, 3g fiber), 6g pro.*

TAKES 30 min.   **SERVES** 4

HACK IT!

Goodbye, Silk
Your produce brush is a handy tool for scrubbing corn silks off the cob. After husking the corn, gently brush each ear under running water, and the silks will come right off.

Air-Fryer Candied Acorn Squash Slices

INGREDIENTS

2 medium acorn squash
⅔ cup packed brown sugar
½ cup butter, softened

DIRECTIONS

Cut squash in half lengthwise; remove and discard seeds. Cut each half crosswise into ½-in. slices; discard ends.

In batches, arrange squash slices in a single layer on greased Crisper Tray. Slide the Crisper Tray into Shelf Position 4. Turn the Function Dial to Air Fry, set temperature to 350° and set timer to 15 minutes. Cook until just tender, 5 minutes per side. Combine sugar and butter; spread over squash. Cook 3 minutes longer. Reset timer to 15 minutes for each batch.

1 SERVING *320 cal., 16g fat (10g sat. fat), 41mg chol., 135mg sod., 48g carb. (29g sugars, 3g fiber), 2g pro.*

PREP 15 min.   **COOK** 15 min./batch   **SERVES** 6

Lemon-Garlic Mushrooms

INGREDIENTS

- ¼ cup lemon juice
- 3 Tbsp. minced fresh parsley
- 2 Tbsp. olive oil
- 3 garlic cloves, minced
  Pepper to taste
- 1 lb. large fresh mushrooms

DIRECTIONS

Slide the Grill Plate into Shelf Position 6. Turn the Function Dial to Air Fry/Grill, set the temperature to 400° and set timer to 25 minutes. Let the grill preheat 10 minutes.

Meanwhile, for dressing, whisk together first 5 ingredients. Toss mushrooms with 2 Tbsp. dressing. When grill has preheated, place mushrooms on Grill Plate and grill until tender, 5-7 minutes per side. Toss mushrooms with remaining dressing before serving.

1 SERVING *94 cal., 7g fat (1g sat. fat), 0 chol., 2mg sod., 6g carb. (0 sugars, 0 fiber), 3g pro.*

TAKES 20 min.   **SERVES** 4

De-Stem Fresh Herbs Quickly

To remove parsley and cilantro leaves quickly and easily, run a fork along the stem. This will gently remove the leaves. You can then mince the herbs in dishes like this one. Other choices include giving them a rough chop—or using whole leaves for a rustic presentation—for favorite dishes.

Air-Fryer Herb & Lemon Cauliflower

INGREDIENTS

- 1 medium head cauliflower, cut into florets (about 6 cups)
- 4 Tbsp. olive oil, divided
- ¼ cup minced fresh parsley
- 1 Tbsp. minced fresh rosemary
- 1 Tbsp. minced fresh thyme
- 1 tsp. grated lemon zest
- 2 Tbsp. lemon juice
- ½ tsp. salt
- ¼ tsp. crushed red pepper flakes

DIRECTIONS

In a large bowl, combine cauliflower and 2 Tbsp. oil; toss to coat. In batches, arrange cauliflower in a single layer on Crisper Tray. Slide the Crisper Tray into Shelf Position 4. Turn the Function Dial to Air Fry, set the temperature to 350° and set timer to 10 minutes. Cook until florets are tender and edges are browned, 8-10 minutes, stirring halfway through. Reset timer to 10 minutes for each batch.

In a small bowl, combine remaining ingredients; stir in remaining 2 Tbsp. oil. Transfer cauliflower to a large bowl; drizzle with herb mixture and toss to combine.

¾ **CUP** *161 cal., 14g fat (2g sat. fat), 0 chol., 342mg sod., 8g carb. (3g sugars, 3g fiber), 3g pro.*

TAKES 30 min. **SERVES** 4

Save Thyme

Getting all the small leaves off a spring of fresh thyme can be tricky, but not anymore. Simply thread a stem through a hole in a colander. This will remove every tiny bit of thyme while collecting it inside the strainer.

Air-Fryer Lemon-Parmesan Asparagus

INGREDIENTS

- ¼ cup mayonnaise
- 4 tsp. olive oil
- 1½ tsp. grated lemon zest
- 1 garlic clove, minced
- ½ tsp. pepper
- ¼ tsp. seasoned salt
- 1 lb. fresh asparagus, trimmed
- 2 Tbsp. shredded Parmesan cheese
  Lemon wedges, optional

DIRECTIONS

In a large bowl, combine the first 6 ingredients. Add asparagus; toss to coat.

In batches, place the asparagus in a single layer on greased Crisper Tray. Slide the Crisper Tray into Shelf Position 4. Turn the Function Dial to Air Fry, set the temperature to 375° and set timer to 10 minutes. Cook until tender and lightly browned, 4-6 minutes. Reset timer as needed for batches. Transfer asparagus to a serving platter; sprinkle with Parmesan cheese. If desired, serve with lemon wedges.

1 SERVING *156 cal., 15g fat (3g sat. fat), 3mg chol., 214mg sod., 3g carb. (1g sugars, 1g fiber), 2g pro.*

TAKES 20 min. **SERVES** 4

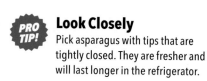

PRO TIP!

Look Closely
Pick asparagus with tips that are tightly closed. They are fresher and will last longer in the refrigerator.

Air-Fryer Parmesan Breaded Squash

INGREDIENTS

- 4 cups thinly sliced yellow summer squash (3 medium)
- 3 Tbsp. olive oil
- ½ tsp. salt
- ½ tsp. pepper
- ⅛ tsp. cayenne pepper
- ¾ cup panko bread crumbs
- ¾ cup grated Parmesan cheese

DIRECTIONS

Place squash in a large bowl. Add oil and seasonings; toss to coat.

In a shallow bowl, mix bread crumbs and cheese. Dip squash in crumb mixture to coat both sides, patting to help coating adhere. In batches, arrange squash in a single layer on Crisper Tray. Slide the Crisper Tray into Shelf Position 4. Turn the Function Dial to Air Fry, set the temperature to 350° and set timer to 10 minutes.

Cook until squash is tender and coating is golden brown, about 10 minutes. Reset timer for each batch.

½ CUP *203 cal., 14g fat (3g sat. fat), 11mg chol., 554mg sod., 13g carb. (4g sugars, 2g fiber), 6g pro.*

PREP 15 min.　　**COOK** 10 min./batch　　**SERVES** 4

Air-Fryer Red Potatoes

INGREDIENTS

- 2 lbs. small unpeeled red potatoes, cut into wedges
- 2 Tbsp. olive oil
- 1 Tbsp. minced fresh rosemary or 1 tsp. dried rosemary, crushed
- 2 garlic cloves, minced
- ½ tsp. salt
- ¼ tsp. pepper

DIRECTIONS

Drizzle potatoes with oil. Sprinkle with rosemary, minced garlic, salt and pepper; toss gently to coat.

Place potatoes on ungreased Crisper Tray. Slide the Crisper Tray into Shelf Position 4. Turn the Function Dial to Air Fry, set the temperature to 400° and set timer to 12 minutes. Cook until potatoes are golden brown and tender, 10-12 minutes, stirring once.

1 CUP *98 cal., 2g fat (0 sat. fat), 0 chol., 155mg sod., 18g carb. (1g sugars, 2g fiber), 2g pro.*

TAKES 20 min.   **SERVES** 8

Air-Fryer Sweet Potato Fries

INGREDIENTS

- 2 large sweet potatoes, cut into thin strips
- 2 Tbsp. canola oil
- 1 tsp. garlic powder
- 1 tsp. paprika
- 1 tsp. kosher salt
- ¼ tsp. cayenne pepper

DIRECTIONS

Combine all ingredients; toss to coat. Place on greased Crisper Tray. Slide Crisper Tray into Shelf Position 4. Turn the Function Dial to Air Fry, set the temperature to 400° and set timer to 12 minutes. Cook until lightly browned, 10-12 minutes, stirring once. Serve immediately.

1 SERVING *243 cal., 7g fat (1g sat. fat), 0 chol., 498mg sod., 43g carb. (17g sugars, 5g fiber), 3g pro.*

TAKES 20 min.   **SERVES** 4

Instant Steak Fries

Whether you're making sweet potato fries or the regular variety, use an apple slicer to cut them steak fries-style. Cut 1 end of the potato for stability. Stand the potato upright, place the apple slicer on top and gently push down. Presto!

Lime & Sesame Grilled Eggplant

INGREDIENTS

- 3 Tbsp. lime juice
- 1 Tbsp. sesame oil
- 1½ tsp. reduced-sodium soy sauce
- 1 garlic clove, minced
- ½ tsp. grated fresh gingerroot or ¼ tsp. ground ginger
- ½ tsp. salt
- ⅛ tsp. pepper
- 1 medium eggplant (1¼ lbs.), cut lengthwise into ½-in. slices
- 2 tsp. honey
- ⅛ tsp. crushed red pepper flakes Thinly sliced green onion and sesame seeds

DIRECTIONS

In a small bowl, whisk first 7 ingredients until blended; brush 2 Tbsp. juice mixture over both sides of eggplant slices. Slide the Grill Plate into Shelf Position 6. Turn the Function Dial to Grill, set the temperature to 425° and set timer to 20 minutes. Let the grill preheat for 5 minutes.

Place eggplant on Grill Plate, in batches if necessary, and grill until tender, 4-6 minutes on each side.

Transfer grilled eggplant to a serving plate. Stir honey and pepper flakes into remaining juice mixture; drizzle over eggplant. Sprinkle with sliced green onion and sesame seeds.

1 SERVING *50 cal., 2g fat (0 sat. fat), 0 chol., 246mg sod., 7g carb. (4g sugars, 2g fiber), 1g pro.*

TAKES 30 min. **SERVES** 6

Bigger Isn't Better

Select the smallest eggplants you can find. The smaller their size, the less bitter they are.

Air-Fried Favorites

Air-Fryer Cheeseburger Onion Rings

INGREDIENTS

- 1 lb. lean ground beef (90% lean)
- ⅓ cup ketchup
- 2 Tbsp. prepared mustard
- ½ tsp. salt
- 1 large onion
- 4 oz. cheddar cheese, cut into squares
- ¾ cup all-purpose flour
- 2 tsp. garlic powder
- 1½ cups panko bread crumbs
- 2 large eggs, lightly beaten
- Cooking spray
- Spicy ketchup, optional

DIRECTIONS

In a small bowl, combine beef, ketchup, mustard and salt, mixing lightly but thoroughly. Cut onion into ½-in. slices; separate into rings. Fill 8 large rings with half of the beef mixture (save remaining onion rings for another use). Top each with a piece of cheese and remaining beef mixture.

In a shallow bowl, mix flour and garlic powder. Place bread crumbs and eggs in separate shallow bowls. Dip filled onion rings into flour to coat both sides; shake off excess. Dip into egg, then into bread crumbs, patting to help coating adhere.

In batches, place onion rings in a single layer on greased Crisper Tray; spritz with cooking spray. Slide the Crisper Tray into Shelf Position 4. Turn the Function Dial to Air Fry, set temperature to 325° and set timer to 15 minutes. Cook each batch until golden brown and a thermometer inserted into beef reads 160°, 12-15 minutes. If desired, serve with spicy ketchup.

1 ONION RING *258 cal., 11g fat (5g sat. fat), 96mg chol., 489mg sod., 19g carb. (4g sugars, 1g fiber), 19g pro.*

PREP 25 min. **COOK** 15 min./batch **SERVES** 8

Air-Fryer Pickles

INGREDIENTS

- 32 dill pickle slices
- ½ cup all-purpose flour
- ½ tsp. salt
- 3 large eggs, lightly beaten
- 2 Tbsp. dill pickle juice
- ½ tsp. cayenne pepper
- ½ tsp. garlic powder
- 2 cups panko bread crumbs
- 2 Tbsp. minced fresh cilantro
- Olive oil cooking spray
- Ranch salad dressing, optional

DIRECTIONS

Let pickles stand on a paper towel until liquid is almost absorbed, about 15 minutes.

Meanwhile, in a shallow bowl, combine flour and salt. In another shallow bowl, whisk eggs, pickle juice, cayenne and garlic powder. Combine panko and cilantro in a third shallow bowl. Dip pickles into flour mixture to coat both sides; shake off excess. Dip into egg mixture, then into crumb mixture, patting to help coating adhere. Spritz pickles with olive oil spray.

Arrange half the pickles in a single layer on the Crisper Tray. Slide Crisper Tray into Shelf Position 4. Turn the Function Dial to Air Fry, set the temperature to 400° and set timer to 20 minutes. Cook 5-7 minutes. Turn pickles over and spritz with olive oil spray. Cook until golden brown and crispy, 7-10 minutes longer. Repeat with remaining pickles. Serve immediately. If desired, serve with ranch dressing.

4 PICKLE SLICES *104 cal., 2g fat (1 sat. fat), 53mg chol., 462mg sod., 15g carb. (1 sugars, 1 fiber), 5g pro.*

PREP 20 min. + standing	**COOK** 15 min./batch
	SERVES 8

Air-Fryer Bacon-Wrapped Avocado Wedges

INGREDIENTS

2 medium ripe avocados
12 bacon strips

SAUCE
½ cup mayonnaise
2 to 3 Tbsp. Sriracha chili sauce
1 to 2 Tbsp. lime juice
1 tsp. grated lime zest

DIRECTIONS

Cut each avocado in half; remove pit and peel. Cut each half into 3 wedges. Wrap 1 bacon slice around each avocado wedge.

Working in batches, place wedges in a single layer in Crisper Tray. Slide the Crisper Tray into Shelf Position 4. Turn Function Dial to Air Fry, set temperature to 400° and set timer to 15 minutes. Cook until bacon is crisp, 10-15 minutes. Reset timer for each batch.

Meanwhile, in a small bowl, stir together mayonnaise, Sriracha sauce, lime juice and lime zest. Serve wedges with sauce.

1 WEDGE *142 cal., 13g fat (3g sat. fat), 9mg chol., 274mg sod., 3g carb. (1g sugars, 2g fiber), 3g pro.*

TAKES 30 min.   **SERVES** 12

PDQ Avocados

When life hands you hard avocados, here's how to ripen them ASAP. Place the avocados in a paper bag with an apple or banana. Poke the bag a few times with a toothpick or scissors and let it sit at room temp for a day or two. The more fruits in the bag (and ethylene gas they give off), the faster the ripening. Once avocado is cut, place it in a container with a few pieces of raw onion, and seal. Sulfur fumes from the onions help stop discoloration.

Air-Fryer Chickpea Fritters with Sweet-Spicy Sauce

INGREDIENTS

- 1 cup plain yogurt
- 2 Tbsp. sugar
- 1 Tbsp. honey
- ½ tsp. salt
- ½ tsp. pepper
- ½ tsp. crushed red pepper flakes

FRITTERS

- 1 can (15 oz.) chickpeas or garbanzo beans, rinsed and drained
- 1 tsp. ground cumin
- ½ tsp. salt
- ½ tsp. garlic powder
- ½ tsp. ground ginger
- 1 large egg
- ½ tsp. baking soda
- ½ cup chopped fresh cilantro
- 2 green onions, thinly sliced

DIRECTIONS

In a small bowl, combine the first 6 ingredients; refrigerate until serving.

Place chickpeas and seasonings in a food processor; process until finely ground. Add egg and baking soda; pulse until blended. Transfer to a bowl; stir in cilantro and green onions.

In batches, drop the chickpea mixture by rounded tablespoonfuls onto greased Crisper Tray. Slide the Crisper Tray into Shelf Position 4. Turn the Function Dial to Air Fry, set the temperature to 400° and set timer to 10 minutes. Cook until lightly browned, 5-6 minutes. Reset timer for each batch. Serve fritters with sauce.

3 FRITTERS WITH 2 TBSP. SAUCE *101 cal., 3g fat (1 sat. fat), 27mg chol., 467mg sod., 16g carb. (8g sugars, 2g fiber), 4g pro.*

PREP 20 min.	**COOK** 5 min./batch	**SERVES** 8

Air-Fryer General Tso's Cauliflower

INGREDIENTS

- ½ cup all-purpose flour
- ½ cup cornstarch
- 1 tsp. salt
- 1 tsp. baking powder
- ¾ cup club soda
- 1 medium head cauliflower, cut into 1-in. florets (about 6 cups)

SAUCE

- ¼ cup orange juice
- 3 Tbsp. sugar
- 3 Tbsp. soy sauce
- 3 Tbsp. vegetable broth
- 2 Tbsp. rice vinegar
- 2 tsp. sesame oil
- 2 tsp. cornstarch
- 2 Tbsp. canola oil
- 2 to 6 dried pasilla or other hot chiles, chopped
- 3 green onions, white part minced, green part thinly sliced, divided
- 3 garlic cloves, minced
- 1 tsp. grated fresh gingerroot
- ½ tsp. grated orange zest
- 4 cups hot cooked rice

DIRECTIONS

Combine flour, cornstarch, salt and baking powder. Stir in club soda just until blended (batter will be thin). Toss florets in batter; transfer to a wire rack set over a baking sheet. Let stand 5 minutes. In batches, place cauliflower on greased Crisper Tray. Slide the Crisper Tray into Shelf Position 4. Turn the Function Dial to Air Fry, set the temperature to 400° and set timer to 12 minutes. Cook each batch until golden brown and tender, 10-12 minutes.

Meanwhile, whisk together first 6 sauce ingredients; whisk in cornstarch until smooth.

In a large saucepan, heat canola oil over medium-high heat. Add desired amount of chiles; cook and stir until fragrant, 1-2 minutes. Add white part of onions, garlic, ginger and orange zest; cook until fragrant, about 1 minute. Stir orange juice mixture; add to pan. Bring to a boil; cook and stir until thickened, 2-4 minutes.

Add cauliflower to sauce; toss to coat. Serve with rice; sprinkle with thinly sliced green onions.

1 CUP CAULIFLOWER WITH 1 CUP RICE *528 cal., 11g fat (1g sat. fat), 0 chol., 1614mg sod., 97g carb. (17g sugars, 5g fiber), 11g pro.*

PREP 25 min.   **COOK** 20 min.   **SERVES** 4

Air-Fryer Pigs in a Poncho

INGREDIENTS

- 8 hot dogs
- 1 can (16 oz.) refried beans
- 8 flour tortillas (10 in.)
- 1 can (4 oz.) chopped green chiles
- 1 can (2¼ oz.) sliced ripe olives, drained
- 2 cups shredded Monterey Jack cheese
  Cooking spray
  Optional: Sour cream and salsa

DIRECTIONS

Slide the Grill Plate into Shelf Position 6. Turn the Function Dial to Grill, set the temperature to 350, and set the timer to 20 minutes. Let the grill preheat for 10 minutes. When the grill has preheated, place the hot dogs on the Grill Plate. Cook until browned and heated through, 4-5 minutes on each side.

Spread beans over center of each tortilla; layer with green chiles, olives and cheese. Place hot dog down center of tortilla. Fold bottom and sides of tortilla over filling and roll up.

In batches, arrange wraps in a single layer on greased Crisper Tray; spritz with cooking spray. Slide the Crisper Tray into Shelf Position 4. Turn the Function Dial to Air Fry, set the temperature to 375° and set timer to 20 minutes. Cook until lightly browned, 6-8 minutes. Turn; spritz with cooking spray. Cook until golden brown and crisp, 6-8 minutes longer. Reset timer for each batch. If desired, serve with sour cream and salsa.

1 WRAP *539 cal., 30g fat (14g sat. fat), 50mg chol., 1486mg sod., 46g carb. (4g sugars, 5g fiber), 21g pro.*

PREP 25 min.   **COOK** 15 min./batch   **SERVES** 8

Air-Fryer Crispy Sriracha Spring Rolls

INGREDIENTS

- 3 cups coleslaw mix (about 7 oz.)
- 3 green onions, chopped
- 1 Tbsp. soy sauce
- 1 tsp. sesame oil
- 1 lb. boneless skinless chicken breasts
- 1 tsp. seasoned salt
- 2 pkg. (8 oz. each) cream cheese, softened
- 2 Tbsp. Sriracha chili sauce
- 24 spring roll wrappers
  Cooking spray
  Optional: Sweet chili sauce and sliced green onions

DIRECTIONS

Toss coleslaw mix, green onions, soy sauce and sesame oil; let stand. Place chicken in a single layer on greased Crisper Tray. Slide the Crisper Tray into Shelf Position 4. Turn the Function Dial to Air Fry, set the temperature to 360° and set the timer to 20 minutes. Cook until a thermometer inserted in the chicken reads 165°, 18-20 minutes. Remove chicken; cool slightly. Finely chop chicken; toss with seasoned salt.

In a large bowl, mix cream cheese and Sriracha chili sauce; stir in chicken and coleslaw mixture. With 1 corner of a spring roll wrapper facing you, place about 2 Tbsp. filling just below center of wrapper. (Cover remaining wrappers with a damp paper towel until ready to use.) Fold bottom corner over filling; moisten remaining edges with water. Fold side corners toward center over filling; roll up tightly, pressing tip to seal. Repeat.

Increase temperature to 400°. In batches, arrange spring rolls in a single layer on greased Crisper Tray; spritz with cooking spray. Set timer to 12 minutes; Cook until lightly browned, 5-6 minutes. Turn; spritz with cooking spray. Cook until golden brown and crisp, 5-6 minutes longer. Reset timer for each batch. Serve warm, with chili sauce and green onions if desired.

2 SPRING ROLLS *254 cal., 15g fat (8g sat. fat), 59mg chol., 429mg sod., 19g carb. (3g sugars, 0 fiber), 12g pro.*

PREP 50 min. **COOK** 10 min./batch **SERVES** 12

Make Ahead

Freeze uncooked spring rolls 1 in. apart in freezer containers, separating the layers with waxed paper. Then, when you want a fast snack or appetizer, cook the frozen spring rolls as directed, increasing the cooking time as necessary.

Air-Fryer Sweet Potato-Crusted Chicken Nuggets

INGREDIENTS

- 1 cup sweet potato chips
- ¼ cup all-purpose flour
- 1 tsp. salt, divided
- ½ tsp. coarsely ground pepper
- ¼ tsp. baking powder
- 1 Tbsp. cornstarch
- 1 lb. chicken tenderloins, cut into 1½-in. pieces
- Cooking spray

DIRECTIONS

Place chips, flour, ½ tsp. salt, pepper and baking powder in a food processor; pulse until ground. Transfer to a shallow dish.

Mix cornstarch and remaining ½ tsp. salt; toss with the chicken. Toss chicken with potato chip mixture, pressing to coat.

In batches, arrange chicken in a single layer on greased Crisper Tray; spritz with cooking spray. Slide the Crisper Tray into Shelf Position 4. Turn the Function Dial to Air Fry, set the temperature to 400° and set timer to 10 minutes. Cook until lightly browned, 3-4 minutes. Turn; spritz with cooking spray. Cook until golden brown and chicken is no longer pink, 3-4 minutes longer. Reset timer for each batch.

3 OZ. COOKED CHICKEN *190 cal., 4g fat (0 sat. fat), 56mg chol., 690mg sod., 13g carb. (1g sugars, 1g fiber), 28g pro.*

PREP 15 min.   **COOK** 10 min./batch   **SERVES** 4

Air-Fryer Peach-Bourbon Wings

INGREDIENTS

- ½ cup peach preserves
- 1 Tbsp. brown sugar
- 1 garlic clove, minced
- ¼ tsp. salt
- 2 Tbsp. white vinegar
- 2 Tbsp. bourbon
- 1 tsp. cornstarch
- 1½ tsp. water
- 2 lbs. chicken wings

DIRECTIONS

Place preserves, brown sugar, garlic and salt in a food processor; process until blended. Transfer to a small saucepan. Add vinegar and bourbon; bring to a boil. Reduce the heat; simmer, uncovered, until slightly thickened, 4-6 minutes.

In a small bowl, mix cornstarch and water until smooth; stir into preserve mixture. Return to a boil, stirring constantly; cook and stir until thickened, 1-2 minutes. Reserve ¼ cup sauce for serving.

Using a sharp knife, cut through the 2 wing joints; discard wing tips. In batches, place wing pieces in a single layer on greased Crisper Tray. Slide the Crisper Tray into Shelf Position 4. Turn the Function Dial to Air Fry, set the temperature to 400° and set timer to 15 minutes. Cook wings for 6 minutes; turn and brush with preserves mixture. Cook until browned and juices run clear, 6-8 minutes longer. Reset timer for each batch. Serve wings immediately with reserved sauce.

2 CHICKEN WING SECTIONS WITH ABOUT 2 TSP. SAUCE
178 cal., 7g fat (2g sat. fat), 29mg chol., 95mg sod., 13g carb. (12g sugars, 0 fiber), 9g pro.

PREP 30 min.   **COOK** 15 min./batch   **SERVES** 9

Air-Fryer Mini Nutella® Doughnut Holes

INGREDIENTS

- 1 large egg
- 1 Tbsp. water
- 1 tube (16.3 oz.) large refrigerated flaky biscuits (8 count)
- ⅔ cup Nutella®
  Oil for deep-fat frying
  Confectioners' sugar

DIRECTIONS

Whisk egg with water. On a lightly floured surface, roll each biscuit into a 6-in. circle; cut each into 4 wedges. Brush lightly with egg mixture; top each wedge with 1 tsp. Nutella®. Bring up corners over filling; pinch edges firmly to seal.

In batches, arrange the biscuits in a single layer on ungreased Crisper Tray. Slide the Crisper Tray into Shelf Position 4. Turn the Function Dial to Air Fry, set temperature to 300° and set timer to 10 minutes. Cook each batch until golden brown, 8-10 minutes, turning once. Dust with confectioners' sugar; serve warm.

2 DOUGHNUTS *198 cal., 13g fat (2g sat. fat), 12mg chol., 283mg sod., 20g carb. (9g sugars, 1g fiber), 3g pro.*

PREP 30 min.   **COOK** 10 min./batch   **SERVES** 16

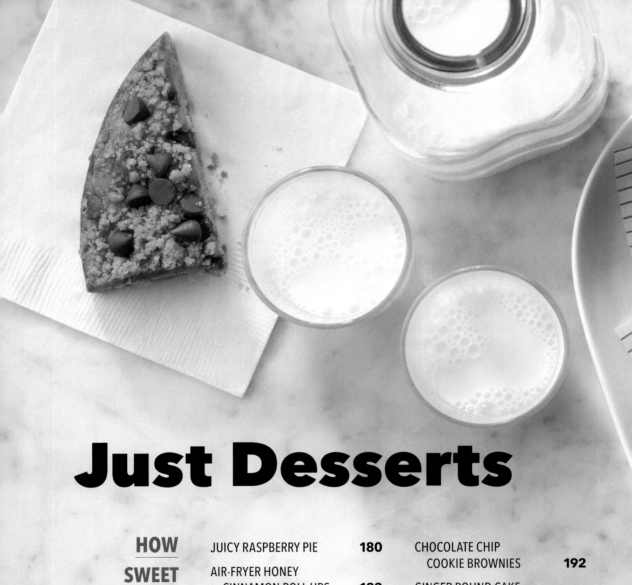

Just Desserts

Juicy Raspberry Pie

INGREDIENTS

2½ cups all-purpose flour
½ tsp. salt
⅔ cup cold unsalted butter, cubed
⅓ cup shortening
6 to 10 Tbsp. ice water

FILLING
5 cups fresh raspberries
2 tsp. lemon juice
¼ tsp. almond extract
1 cup sugar
⅓ cup all-purpose flour
1 tsp. ground cinnamon

SUGAR TOPPING
1 tsp. sugar
¼ tsp. ground cinnamon
1 Tbsp. 2% milk

DIRECTIONS

In a large bowl, mix flour and salt; cut in butter and shortening until crumbly. Gradually add ice water, tossing with a fork until dough holds together when pressed. Divide dough in half. Shape each into a disk; wrap and refrigerate 1 hour or overnight.

For filling, place raspberries in a large bowl; drizzle with lemon juice and almond extract. In a small bowl, mix sugar, flour and cinnamon. Sprinkle over the raspberries and toss gently to coat.

On a lightly floured surface, roll half the dough to a ⅛-in.-thick circle; transfer to a 9-in. pie plate that fits in the unit. Trim crust even with rim. Add filling. Roll remaining dough to a ⅛-in.-thick circle; cut out stars or other shapes using cookie cutters. Place top crust over filling. Trim, seal and flute edge. If desired, decorate top with cutouts.

Slide the Pizza Rack into Shelf Position 5; place the pie on Pizza Rack. Turn the Function Dial to Pizza/Bake, set temperature to 350° and set timer to 40 minutes. For topping, mix sugar and cinnamon. When cycle ends, brush top of hot pie with milk; sprinkle with sugar mixture. Set timer to 20 minutes. Bake pie until crust is golden brown and filling is bubbly, 15-20 minutes longer. Cool on a wire rack.

1 PIECE *520 cal., 24g fat (12g sat. fat), 40mg chol., 151mg sod., 70g carb. (31g sugars, 7g fiber), 6g pro.*

PREP 35 min. + chilling   **BAKE** 55 min. + cooling
SERVES 8

Air-Fryer Honey Cinnamon Roll-Ups

INGREDIENTS

- 2 cups ground walnuts, toasted
- ¼ cup sugar
- 2 tsp. ground cinnamon
- 12 sheets frozen phyllo dough, thawed
- ½ cup butter, melted

SYRUP
- ½ cup honey
- ½ cup sugar
- ½ cup water
- 1 Tbsp. lemon juice

DIRECTIONS

Combine walnuts, sugar and cinnamon. Place 1 sheet of phyllo dough on a 15x12-in. piece of waxed paper; brush with butter. Place a second phyllo sheet on top, brushing it with butter. (Keep the remaining phyllo covered with a damp towel to prevent it from drying out.) Sprinkle with ¼ cup walnut mixture. Using the waxed paper, roll up tightly jelly-roll style, starting with a long side, removing paper as you roll. Slice roll into 4 smaller rolls. Brush with butter; secure with toothpicks. Repeat with remaining phyllo dough and ¼ cupfuls of walnut mixture.

In batches, place roll-ups in a single layer on greased Crisper Tray. Slide Crisper Tray into Shelf Position 4. Turn the Function Dial to Air Fry, set the temperature to 325° and set the timer for 12 minutes.

Cook roll-ups until light brown, 9-11 minutes per batch. Cool on a wire rack. Discard toothpicks.

Meanwhile, in a small saucepan, combine all syrup ingredients. Bring to a boil. Reduce heat; simmer 5 minutes. Cool for 10 minutes. Transfer cinnamon roll-ups to a serving platter; drizzle with syrup. Sprinkle with remaining walnut mixture.

1 CINNAMON ROLL-UP *140 cal., 8g fat (3g sat. fat), 10mg chol., 56mg sod., 17g carb. (13g sugars, 1g fiber), 2g pro.*

PREP 35 min. + cooling **COOK** 10 min./batch
SERVES 24

Grilled Banana Brownie Sundaes

INGREDIENTS

- 2 medium bananas, unpeeled
- 4 oz. cream cheese, softened
- ¼ cup packed brown sugar
- 3 Tbsp. creamy peanut butter
- 8 prepared brownies (2-in. squares)
- 4 cups vanilla ice cream
- ½ cup hot fudge ice cream topping, warmed
- ½ cup chopped salted peanuts

DIRECTIONS

Slide the Grill Plate into Shelf Position 6. Turn the Function Dial to Grill, set temperature to 375° and set timer to 12 minutes. Preheat grill for 5 minutes.

Meanwhile, cut unpeeled bananas crosswise in half, then lengthwise in half. When the Grill Plate is preheated, place quartered bananas on Grill Plate, cut side down. Grill until lightly browned, 2-3 minutes per side. Cool slightly.

In a small bowl, beat cream cheese, brown sugar and peanut butter until smooth. To serve, remove bananas from peel; place over brownies. Top with cream cheese mixture, ice cream, fudge topping and peanuts.

1 SERVING *505 cal., 28g fat (11g sat. fat), 62mg chol., 277mg sod., 57g carb. (33g sugars, 3g fiber), 10g pro.*

TAKES 15 min.   **SERVES** 8

WHO KNEW? **Clean Start**
Wash your fruit before eating or cooking with it. This includes rinds on melons and peels on citrus fruits and bananas. If you cut an unwashed melon, any microorganisms on the rind will be transferred to the flesh as the knife passes through the fruit. The same holds true for citrus fruits and bananas. What's on the skin can be transferred to the fruit as it is peeled, so take a few extra minutes to be safe.

Down East Blueberry Buckle

INGREDIENTS

- 2 cups all-purpose flour
- ¾ cup sugar
- 2½ tsp. baking powder
- ¼ tsp. salt
- 1 large egg, room temperature
- ¾ cup 2% milk
- ¼ cup butter, melted
- 2 cups fresh or frozen blueberries

TOPPING
- ½ cup sugar
- ⅓ cup all-purpose flour
- ½ tsp. ground cinnamon
- ¼ cup butter, softened

DIRECTIONS

In a large bowl, whisk flour, sugar, baking powder and salt. In another bowl, whisk egg, milk and melted butter until blended. Add to flour mixture; stir just until moistened. Fold in blueberries. Transfer to a greased 9-in. square baking pan that fits in the unit.

For topping, in a small bowl, mix sugar, flour and cinnamon. Using a fork, stir in softened butter until mixture is crumbly. Sprinkle over batter.

Slide the Pizza Rack into Shelf Position 5. Place the baking pan on the Pizza Rack. Turn the Function Dial to Pizza/Bake, set the temperature to 375° and set the timer to 30 minutes. Bake until a toothpick inserted in center comes out clean, 25-30 minutes (do not overbake). Cool in pan on a wire rack. Serve warm or at room temperature.

1 PIECE *354 cal., 12g fat (7g sat. fat), 49mg chol., 277mg sod., 59g carb. (32g sugars, 2g fiber), 5g pro.*

PREP 15 min.   **BAKE** 25 min.   **SERVES** 9

Washing Can Wait
Don't wash blueberries more than 1 day ahead of using them, or they may mold.

Bacon Chocolate Chip Cheesecake Blondies

INGREDIENTS

- 8 bacon strips, cooked and crumbled
- 1 cup butter, softened
- ¾ cup sugar
- ¾ cup packed brown sugar
- 2 large eggs, room temperature
- 1 tsp. vanilla extract
- 2¼ cups all-purpose flour
- 1 tsp. salt
- 1 tsp. baking soda
- 2 cups (12 oz.) semisweet chocolate chips

CHEESECAKE LAYER

- 2 pkg. (8 oz. each) cream cheese, softened
- 1 cup sugar
- 2 large eggs, room temperature
- ¾ cup 2% milk
- 2 tsp. vanilla extract

DIRECTIONS

Line a 9-in. square baking pan that fits in the unit with foil, letting ends extend up sides; grease foil.

Reserve ¼ cup crumbled bacon for top. In a large bowl, cream butter and sugars until light and fluffy. Beat in eggs and vanilla. In another bowl, whisk flour, salt and baking soda; gradually beat into creamed mixture. Stir in chocolate chips and remaining bacon. Press half the dough onto bottom of prepared pan.

For cheesecake layer, in a large bowl, beat cream cheese and sugar until smooth. Add eggs, milk and vanilla; beat on low speed just until blended. Pour over dough in prepared pan; drop remaining dough by rounded tablespoonfuls over cheesecake layer. Sprinkle with reserved bacon.

Slide the Pizza Rack into Shelf Position 5. Place the baking pan on the Pizza Rack. Turn the Function Dial to Pizza/Bake, set the temperature to 375° and set the timer to 45 minutes. Bake until golden brown and cheesecake has set, 40-45 minutes; cool in pan on a wire rack. Refrigerate at least 4 hours before cutting. Lifting with foil, remove from pan. Cut into bars.

1 BAR *534 cal., 31g fat (18g sat. fat), 113mg chol., 523mg sod., 61g carb. (45g sugars, 2g fiber), 8g pro.*

| PREP 30 min. | BAKE 40 min. + chilling | SERVES 16 |

Get Things Settled

Next time you open a new bag of flour, save some mess with this trick. Slap the top of the bag a couple of times before opening it. This settles the flour so it doesn't spray out when you open the bag.

Air-Fryer Lemon Slice Sugar Cookies

INGREDIENTS

- ½ cup unsalted butter, softened
- 1 pkg. (3.4 oz.) instant lemon pudding mix
- ½ cup sugar
- 1 large egg, room temperature
- 2 Tbsp. 2% milk
- 1½ cups all-purpose flour
- 1 tsp. baking powder
- ¼ tsp. salt

ICING
- ⅔ cup confectioners' sugar
- 2 to 4 tsp. lemon juice

DIRECTIONS

In a large bowl, cream butter, pudding mix and sugar until light and fluffy, 5-7 minutes. Beat in egg and milk. In another bowl, whisk flour, baking powder and salt; gradually beat into creamed mixture.

Divide dough in half. On a lightly floured surface, shape each into a 6-in.-long roll. Wrap and refrigerate 3 hours or until firm.

Unwrap and cut dough crosswise into ½-in. slices. In batches, place slices in a single layer on greased Crisper Tray. Slide Crisper Tray into Shelf Position 4. Turn the Function Dial to Air Fry, set the temperature to 325° and set timer for 12 minutes. Cook each batch until edges are light brown, 8-12 minutes. Cool in tray 2 minutes. Remove to wire racks to cool completely.

In a small bowl, mix confectioners' sugar and enough lemon juice to reach a drizzling consistency. Drizzle over cookies. Let stand until set.

1 COOKIE *110 cal., 4g fat (2g sat. fat), 18mg chol., 99mg sod., 17g carb. (11g sugars, 0 fiber), 1g pro.*

PREP 15 min. + chilling	**COOK** 10 min./batch
	SERVES 24

PRO TIP!

Make Ahead
Get the cookie dough out of the way up to 2 days in advance. Just place the wrapped dough in a resealable container and store it in the fridge. If you want to freeze the dough for future baking, place the wrapped logs in a resealable container and store it in the freezer. To use, unwrap the frozen logs and cut them into slices. Cook as directed, increasing the time by 1-2 minutes.

Chocolate Chip Cookie Brownies

INGREDIENTS

- ¾ cup butter
- 1½ cups sugar
- ½ cup baking cocoa
- 3 large eggs, room temperature
- ¾ cup all-purpose flour
- ½ cup chopped walnuts

CHOCOLATE CHIP LAYER

- ½ cup butter
- 1 cup packed brown sugar
- 1 large egg, room temperature
- 1 cup all-purpose flour
- ½ tsp. baking soda
- 1 cup semisweet chocolate chips

No-Slip Trick

Need an extra hand in the kitchen? Take a cue from professional chefs and place a damp dish towel under the mixing bowl. This keeps the bowl from sliding away during mixing. It also lets you have a hand free for adding other ingredients. Place a damp towel under a cutting board for the same stability.

DIRECTIONS

Line a 9-in. square baking pan that fits in the unit with foil, letting ends extend up sides; grease foil.

In a microwave, melt butter in a large microwave-safe bowl. Stir in sugar and cocoa. Add eggs, 1 at a time, whisking to blend after each addition. Add flour; stir just until combined. Stir in chopped walnuts. Spread into prepared pan.

Slide the Pizza Rack into Shelf Position 5. Place the baking pan on the Pizza Rack. Turn the Function Dial to Pizza/Bake, set the temperature to 350° and set the timer to 15 minutes.

Meanwhile, for chocolate chip layer, melt butter in another microwave-safe bowl. Stir in brown sugar. Whisk in egg. In a small bowl, whisk flour and baking soda; stir into butter mixture just until combined. Stir in chocolate chips. After the brownie layer has baked for 15 minutes, spoon mixture over the hot layer.

Set timer for 40 minutes; bake until a toothpick inserted in center comes out with moist crumbs, 35-40 minutes. Cool completely in pan on a wire rack. Lifting foil, remove brownies from pan. Cut into bars.

1 BROWNIE *536 cal., 29g fat (15g sat. fat), 113mg chol., 236mg sod., 69g carb. (51g sugars, 2g fiber), 6g pro.*

| **PREP** 15 min. | **BAKE** 50 min. + cooling | **SERVES** 12 |

Ginger Pound Cake S'mores

INGREDIENTS

- 8 large marshmallows
- 5 oz. bittersweet chocolate candy bars, broken into 8 pieces
- 8 tsp. crystallized ginger
- 16 slices pound cake (¼ in. thick)
- 3 Tbsp. butter, softened

DIRECTIONS

Cut each marshmallow lengthwise into 4 slices. Place a chocolate piece, 4 marshmallow slices and 1 tsp. crystallized ginger on each of 8 cake slices; top with remaining cake. Spread outsides of cake slices with butter.

Slide the Grill Plate into Shelf Position 6. Turn the Function Dial to Grill, set the temperature to 375° and set the timer to 10 minutes. Preheat the grill for 5 minutes. Place cake stacks on Grill Plate and grill each side until toasted, 1-2 minutes on each side.

1 S'MORE *382 cal., 24g fat (13g sat. fat), 144mg chol., 272mg sod., 44g carb. (10g sugars, 2g fiber), 5g pro.*

TAKES 20 min.   **SERVES** 8

Air-Fryer Honeyed Pears in Puff Pastry

INGREDIENTS

4 small pears
4 cups water
2 cups sugar
1 cup honey
1 small lemon, halved
3 cinnamon sticks (3 in.)
6 to 8 whole cloves
1 vanilla bean
1 sheet frozen puff pastry, thawed
1 large egg, lightly beaten

DIRECTIONS

Core pears from bottom, leaving stems intact. Peel pears; cut ¼ in. from the bottom to level if necessary.

In a large saucepan, combine water, sugar, honey, lemon halves, cinnamon and cloves. Split the vanilla bean and scrape seeds; add bean and seeds to sugar mixture. Bring to a boil. Reduce heat; place pears on their sides in saucepan and poach, uncovered, until almost tender, basting occasionally with poaching liquid, 16-20 minutes. Remove pears with a slotted spoon; cool slightly. Strain and reserve 1½ cups poaching liquid; set aside.

Unfold puff pastry on a lightly floured surface. Cut into ½-in.-wide strips. Brush lightly with beaten egg. Starting at the bottom of a pear, wrap a pastry strip around pear, adding strips until pear is completely wrapped. Repeat with remaining pears and puff pastry.

Place pears in a single layer on greased Crisper Tray. Slide Crisper Tray into Shelf Position 4. Turn the Function Dial to Air Fry, set the temperature to 325° and set the timer for 15 minutes. Cook until golden brown, 12-15 minutes. Meanwhile, bring reserved poaching liquid to a boil; cook until liquid is thick and syrupy, about 10 minutes. Place the pears on dessert plates and drizzle with syrup. Serve warm.

1 PEAR WITH 3 TBSP. SYRUP *536 cal., 18g fat (4g sat. fat), 47mg chol., 223mg sod., 92g carb. (50g sugars, 9g fiber), 7g pro.*

PREP 25 min.   **COOK** 15 min.   **SERVES** 4

PRO TIP!
Year-Round Treat
Pears are available all year, but peak season is July through January.

Grilled Figgy Pies

INGREDIENTS

- 2 sheets refrigerated pie crust
- 12 dried figs
- ¼ cup bourbon
- ½ cup chopped walnuts
- ¼ cup plus 1 Tbsp. maple syrup, divided
- 1 tsp. ground cinnamon
- ½ tsp. ground nutmeg
- ½ tsp. vanilla extract
- ⅔ cup (about 5 oz.) mascarpone cheese
- 1 large egg
- 1 Tbsp. water

DIRECTIONS

Warm crusts to room temperature according to package directions. Meanwhile, in a small saucepan, combine figs and bourbon; add water to cover by 1 in. Cook, covered, over low heat until figs are plump, 15-20 minutes. Remove from heat; drain. Cool 15 minutes and pat dry. Cut each fig into quarters. Set aside.

In same saucepan over medium-low heat, combine walnuts with ¼ cup maple syrup, cinnamon and nutmeg. Cook, stirring constantly, until liquid is almost evaporated, 5-7 minutes. Spread nuts on a parchment-lined baking sheet; freeze until set, about 10 minutes.

Unroll crusts. Using a 4-in. round cutter, cut 12 circles, rolling and cutting scraps as necessary. Stir vanilla and remaining 1 Tbsp. maple syrup into mascarpone cheese. Spread scant 1 Tbsp. mascarpone mixture over half of each circle to within ¼ in. of edge; layer with 2 tsp. maple walnuts and 4 fig pieces. Whisk egg and water; moisten edge of crust. Fold crust over filling; press edges with a fork to seal. Repeat with remaining crusts and filling. Brush egg wash over pies. Freeze pies on a parchment-lined baking sheet 10 minutes.

Slide the Grill Plate into Shelf Position 6. Turn the Function Dial to Grill, set temperature to 375° and timer to 20 minutes. Preheat the grill for 5 minutes. Grill pies until golden brown, 5-7 minutes per side.

1 HAND PIE *280 cal., 17g fat (7g sat. fat), 35mg chol., 137mg sod., 28g carb. (10g sugars, 1g fiber), 4g pro.*

PREP 50 min. + freezing   **GRILL** 10 min.   **SERVES** 12

Air-Fryer Apple Pie Egg Rolls

INGREDIENTS

- 3 cups chopped peeled tart apples
- ½ cup packed light brown sugar
- 2½ tsp. ground cinnamon, divided
- 1 tsp. cornstarch
- 8 egg roll wrappers
- ½ cup spreadable cream cheese
  Butter-flavored cooking spray
- 1 Tbsp. sugar
- ⅔ cup hot caramel ice cream topping

DIRECTIONS

In a small bowl, combine apples, brown sugar, 2 tsp. cinnamon and cornstarch. With a corner of an egg roll wrapper facing you, spread 1 scant Tbsp. cream cheese to within 1 in. of edges. Place ⅓ cup apple mixture just below center of wrapper. (Cover remaining wrappers with a damp paper towel until ready to use.)

Fold bottom corner over filling; moisten remaining wrapper edges with water. Fold side corners toward center over filling. Roll egg roll up tightly, pressing at tip to seal. Repeat.

In batches, arrange egg rolls in a single layer on greased Crisper Tray; spritz with cooking spray. Slide Crisper Tray into Shelf Position 4. Turn Function Dial to Air Fry, set temperature to 400° and set timer for 15 minutes for each batch.

Cook until light golden brown, 5-6 minutes. Turn; spritz with cooking spray. Cook until golden brown and crisp, 5-6 minutes longer. Combine sugar and remaining ½ tsp. cinnamon; roll hot egg rolls in mixture. Serve with caramel sauce.

1 ROLL *273 cal., 4g fat (2g sat. fat), 13mg chol., 343mg sod., 56g carb. (35g sugars, 2g fiber), 5g pro.*

PREP 25 min. **COOK** 10 min./batch **SERVES** 8

Peanut Butter Chocolate Chip Zucchini Cake

INGREDIENTS

- ⅓ cup creamy peanut butter
- ¼ cup butter, softened
- 1 cup packed brown sugar
- 1½ cups all-purpose flour, divided
- ½ tsp. salt
- ½ tsp. baking soda
- 1 large egg, room temperature
- 1 tsp. vanilla extract
- ¼ cup buttermilk
- 1 cup shredded zucchini
- ¼ tsp. ground cinnamon
- ½ cup semisweet chocolate chips

DIRECTIONS

In a large bowl, cream peanut butter, butter and brown sugar until blended. In another bowl, whisk 1¼ cups flour, salt and baking soda; add to creamed mixture. Beat just until mixture is sandy. Remove ½ cup crumb mixture for topping.

To remaining mixture, beat in remaining flour, egg, vanilla and buttermilk. Stir in zucchini. Spread into a greased 9-in. round baking pan that fits in the unit. Stir cinnamon into reserved topping. Sprinkle over batter; top with chocolate chips.

Slide the Pizza Rack into Shelf Position 5. Place the baking pan on the Pizza Rack. Turn the Function Dial to Pizza/Bake, set the temperature to 350° and set the timer to 25 minutes. Bake until a toothpick inserted in center comes out with moist crumbs, 20-25 minutes. Cool in pan on a wire rack.

1 PIECE *297 cal., 12g fat (6g sat. fat), 31mg chol., 281mg sod., 44g carb. (28g sugars, 2g fiber), 5g pro.*

PREP 20 min.   **BAKE** 20 min.   **SERVES** 10

Tasty Surprises

Toast It

We like our bagels lightly toasted, which takes just 3 minutes in your PowerXL Air Fryer Grill. If you like even more golden crunch, add toasting time in 30-second intervals until you're happy.

Spread Out!

WHIP UP A COUPLE OF THESE TOPPINGS AND POP THEM INTO THE FRIDGE THE DAY BEFORE YOUR BRUNCH PARTY. THEN JUST HAVE SOMEONE PICK UP BAGELS ON THE WAY OVER. DONE AND DONE!

1. ORANGE MARMALADE
Combine 1 cup softened **cream cheese** with ⅓ cup **orange marmalade**.

2. MEDITERRANEAN GOAT CHEESE
Combine 1 cup softened **cream cheese,** ⅓ cup **goat cheese,** ¼ cup chopped **olives,** ¼ cup chopped **roasted red peppers** and 2 tsp. grated **lemon zest.** Season with **salt** and **pepper** to taste.

3. INSIDE-OUT "EVERYTHING"
Combine 1 cup **cream cheese,** 1 Tbsp. each **poppy seeds** and **sesame seeds,** 2 tsp. each **dried minced garlic** and **dried minced onion,** and 1 tsp. **Worcestershire sauce.** Season with **salt** and **pepper** to taste.

4. BEER CHEESE
Combine 1 cup softened **cream cheese,** ½ cup shredded **cheddar cheese,** 3 Tbsp. **beer** and ½ envelope **ranch dressing mix.** Add **salt** and **pepper** to taste.

5. PECAN PIE
Combine 1 cup softened **cream cheese,** ½ cup toasted chopped **pecans** and ¼ cup **caramel sauce.**

Air-Fryer Potato Chips

| INGREDIENTS | DIRECTIONS |

INGREDIENTS

2 large potatoes
Olive oil-flavored cooking spray
½ tsp. sea salt
Minced fresh parsley, optional

DIRECTIONS

Using a mandoline or vegetable peeler, cut potatoes into very thin slices. Transfer to a large bowl; add enough ice water to cover. Soak for 15 minutes; drain. Add ice water again and soak for 15 minutes.

Drain potatoes; place on towels and pat dry. Spritz potatoes with cooking spray; sprinkle with salt.

In batches, place potato slices in a single layer in the Crisper Tray. Slide Crisper Tray into Shelf Position 4. Turn the Function Dial to Air Fry, set the temperature to 350° and set the timer to 20 minutes per batch. Cook until crisp and golden brown, 15-17 minutes, stirring and turning every 5 minutes. If desired, sprinkle with fresh parsley.

1 CUP *148 cal., 1g fat (0 sat. fat), 0 chol., 252mg sod., 32g carb. (2g sugars, 4g fiber), 4g pro.*

PREP 30 min.   **COOK** 15 min./batch   **SERVES** 6

EXTRA CRUNCHY

1

SPICY CAJUN CHIPS

Instead of salt, toss uncooked potato chips with **Cajun seasoning** (page 93). Proceed as directed.

2

CHOCOLATE-DRIZZLED POTATO CHIPS

Prepare **potato chips** as directed. After chips have cooled, drizzle chips with melted **semisweet** or **dark chocolate** and sprinkle with **coarse sea salt**. Let stand until set.

3

NACHO POTATO CHIPS

After preparing chips as directed, sprinkle with shredded **cheddar, Colby** or **Monterey Jack cheese** and air fry for 2-3 minutes or until cheese is melted. Top with chopped **green onions** and your favorite **hot sauce** or **salsa**.

Nacho Average Nachos

IT'S NOT A PARTY UNTIL THERE ARE NACHOS. TRY THESE INVENTIVE TAKES TO WOW YOUR CROWD.

1. TEX-MEX STYLE NACHOS
Pulled pork BBQ, coleslaw, BBQ sauce, pickled red onions, nacho cheese and a **sour cream** drizzle!

2. I LOVE A DESSERT NACHOS
Brownie brittle for the chips and **marshmallow fluff** for the nacho cheese. Then drizzle on **chocolate sauce** and top with grated **white chocolate** and **chopped peanuts.**

3. BUFFALO WING NACHOS
Spicy buffalo sauce, celery and **shredded chicken,** finished off with drizzles of both **blue cheese** and **ranch dressing.**

4. GRINDER NACHOS
Italian sausage, mushrooms, onions, pizza sauce (just a little), **scamorza cheese** and **pickled pepper rings.**

The Best Ever Pancakes

INGREDIENTS

1½ cups all-purpose flour
2 Tbsp. sugar
1 tsp. baking powder
½ tsp. baking soda
½ tsp. salt
1 cup buttermilk
2 large eggs, room temperature
¼ cup butter, melted
1 tsp. vanilla extract

DIRECTIONS

In a large bowl, whisk together the first 5 ingredients. In another bowl, whisk remaining ingredients; stir into dry ingredients just until moistened.

Slide the Griddle Plate into Shelf Position 6. Turn the Function Dial to Grill, set temperature to 350° and set timer to 30 minutes. Let the Griddle Plate preheat for 10 minutes. Lightly grease Griddle Plate.

Pour batter by ¼ cupfuls onto Griddle Plate; cook until bubbles on top begin to pop and bottoms are golden brown. Turn; cook until second side is golden brown.

3 PANCAKES *360 cal., 15g fat (8g sat. fat), 126mg chol., 817mg sod., 45g carb. (10g sugars, 1g fiber), 10g pro.*

PREP 15 min.   **COOK** 5 min./batch   **SERVES** 4

TASTY TWISTS

1 **BLUEBERRY-LEMON PANCAKES**
Stir up to 1 cup fresh **blueberries** and 2 tsp. **lemon zest** into the prepared **batter**. Cook as directed.

2 **BACON CORNMEAL PANCAKES**
Replace 3 Tbsp. all-purpose flour with **cornmeal,** stirring in 4 slices of cooked, crumbled **bacon** at the end. Cook as directed.

3 **CHOCOLATE PECAN PANCAKES**
Prepare pancake **batter** as directed, replacing ¼ cup flour with **cocoa powder.** Stir ½ cup chopped toasted **pecans** into prepared batter. Cook as directed.

Bacon-Wrapped Snacks

COMPLEMENTARY FLAVORS COME TOGETHER IN THESE NO-FUSS PARTY PLEASERS.

1. DRIED APRICOTS WRAPPED IN BACON
Bake 'em in the Power XL Air Fryer Grill for about 30 minutes at 350°; turn after 20 minutes. Make a dipping sauce from 1 jar **plum jam** and **soy sauce** to taste; stir over medium-low heat till melted.

2. BACON-Y MEATBALLS
You can use meat loaf goodness to make appetizer bites. (Try the **Mini Meat Loaf** recipe on page 77.) Don't forget to whip up a sweet BBQ sauce for a dip or topping!

3. BACON-WRAPPED ASPARAGUS
Use the grill function and add **lemon zest, salt, pepper** and **maple syrup!**

4. SURF & TURF
Stuff **shrimp** with **Monterey Jack cheese** and wrap in **bacon;** air-fry at 375° until cooked.

5. SPUD LOVERS
Bake small **red potatoes** at 375° until just tender. Cool slightly; cut in wedges. Wrap each with **bacon,** securing with a toothpick. Air-fry at 375° until bacon is crisp. Serve with **sour cream** for dipping.

Grilled Cheese Showdown

INGREDIENTS

- 3 Tbsp. butter, softened, divided
- 4 slices sourdough bread
- 2 Tbsp. mayonnaise
- 1 Tbsp. finely shredded Manchego or Parmesan cheese
- 1/8 tsp. onion powder
- 1/4 cup shredded sharp white cheddar cheese
- 1/4 cup shredded Monterey Jack cheese
- 1/4 cup shredded Gruyere cheese
- 2 oz. Brie cheese, rind removed

DIRECTIONS

Slide the Griddle Plate into Shelf Position 6. Turn the Function Dial to Air Fry/Grill, set the temperature to 400° and set the timer to 30 minutes. Let the grill preheat for 5 minutes. Meanwhile, spread 2 Tbsp. butter on 1 side of bread slices. When the Griddle Plate has preheated, in batches, place the bread, butter side down, on the Griddle Plate. Cook until golden brown, 3-4 minutes; remove.

In a small bowl, mix together mayonnaise, Manchego cheese, onion powder and remaining 1 Tbsp. butter. In another bowl, combine cheddar, Monterey Jack and Gruyere cheeses. Slice Brie.

To assemble sandwiches, top toasted side of 2 bread slices with sliced Brie. Sprinkle cheddar cheese mixture evenly over Brie. Top with remaining bread slices, toasted side down. Spread mayonnaise mixture on the outsides of each sandwich. Place sandwiches on the Griddle Plate. Cook until golden brown and cheese is melted, 4-5 minutes on each side. Serve immediately.

1 SANDWICH *774 cal., 60g fat (32g sat. fat), 150mg chol., 1210mg sod., 30g carb. (3g sugars, 1g fiber), 30g pro.*

TAKES 25 min.   **SERVES** 2

TOP-DOWN DELISH

1

GRILLED CHEESE, HAM & APPLE SANDWICH
Prepare grilled cheese sandwich as directed, adding sliced **deli ham** and sliced **Granny Smith apple** on top of the **Brie.**

2

BERRY GRILLED CHEESE SANDWICH
Prepare grilled cheese sandwich as directed, adding ¼ cup **fresh raspberries** and/or **blackberries** on top of the **Brie.**

3

GRILLED CHEESE, BACON & SUN-DRIED TOMATO SANDWICH
Prepare grilled cheese sandwich as directed, adding slices of crispy **bacon,** julienned **sun-dried tomatoes** and sliced **avocado** on top of the **Brie.**

FROM TOP: Grilled Cheese Showdown; Grilled Cheese, Ham & Apple Sandwich; Berry Grilled Cheese Sandwich; and Grilled Cheese, Bacon & Sun-Dried Tomato Sandwich

Tropical Zing!

USE THE ROTISSERIE PINEAPPLE
RECIPE ON PAGE 102 TO CREATE
THESE SUMMERY TREATS.

1. GOOD MORNING OATMEAL
Brighten up **oatmeal** with wedges
of **pineapple** and a sprinkling of
cinnamon and **ground ginger**.

2. PINEAPPLE SALSA
Finely chop it and mix into your
favorite homemade or jarred **salsa**
to add a sweet and tangy twist.

3. TIKI DOG
Nestle long, thin **pineapple slices**
inside a **hot dog bun** with a grilled
hot dog or **sausage**. Top with a drizzle
of **hoisin sauce** and a sprinkling of
chopped **green onions**.

4. GRILLED POUND CAKE
WITH PINEAPPLE
Grill slices of store-bought or
homemade **pound cake** until lightly
charred. Top with sliced **pineapple**
and a dollop of **whipped cream**.

5. FRUITY SKEWERS
Skewer chunks of **pineapple** with
kiwi and **strawberries** for a garnish
in a refreshing wine like a **Riesling**
or a summer **sangria**.